To Vicky

With admiration

Cato the Younger

GUILTY MEN

GUILTY MEN

by

"CATO THE YOUNGER"

Biteback Publishing

First published in Great Britain in 2017 by
Biteback Publishing Ltd
Westminster Tower
3 Albert Embankment
London SE1 7SP
Copyright © Cato the Younger 2017

ISBN 978-1-78590-241-3

10 9 8 7 6 5 4 3 2 1

A CIP catalogue record for this book is available from the British Library.

Set in Bulmer

Printed and bound in Great Britain by
CPI Group (UK) Ltd, Croydon CR0 4YY

MIX
Paper from
responsible sources
FSC® C020471

FROM PREAMBLE TO *1940 GUILTY MEN*

On a spring day in 1793, a crowd of angry men burst their way through the doors of the assembly room where the French Convention was in session. A discomforted figure addressed them from the rostrum. 'What do the people desire?' he asked. 'The Convention has only their welfare at heart.' The leader of the angry crowd replied, 'The people haven't come here to be given a lot of phrases. They demand a dozen guilty men.'

'The use of recriminating about the past is to enforce effective action at the present.'
– Mr Winston Churchill, 29 May 1936

CATO THE YOUNGER
(MARCUS PORCIUS CATO
UTICENSIS, 95-46BC)

CATO THE YOUNGER WAS born in Rome in 95BC,
the great-grandson of 'Cato the Censor' (234–149BC). Cato
the Younger warned the leaders of Rome about the risks of
folly, specifically the dangers to Rome's customs and traditions from 'degenerate' influences. Cato was renowned as a
politician and orator of virtue and incorruptibility, and a disci-
ple of Stoic philosophy. His parents died when he was a young
child and he was taken in by his uncle, Marcus Livius Drusus.
Cato lived an ascetic lifestyle from a young age, following in
the steps of his famously abstemious great-grandfather. Both
Catos engaged in vigorous, brutal exercise, steeling themselves
for adverse weather conditions and eschewing materialism. In
65BC, Cato the Younger was elected Quaestor, and was widely
praised for his performance. As a Senator, he was driven and

committed, never missing a session of the Senate, and soon carved out a prominent position for himself in the Senate's conservative wing. In 54BC, he was elected as Praetor. But his political career became tainted by conflict with Julius Caesar: it was to be his undoing. Cato angered Caesar during the Catilinarian conspiracy, and thus was a rivalry was born. Cato set himself firmly against the 'triumvirate', composed of Caesar, Pompey and Marcus Licinius Crassus. The old Republic had broken down. Cato the Younger committed suicide.

THE GUILTY MEN

M. François Mitterrand

Herr Helmut Kohl

Baroness Margaret Thatcher

Lord Norman Tebbit

Mr Paul Dacre

Mr Rupert Murdoch

Mr Anthony Blair

Mr Jean-Claude Juncker

Mr Nigel Farage

Mr David Cameron

Frau Angela Merkel

Mr Arron Banks

Mr Dominic Cummings

Mr Boris Johnson

Mr Jeremy Corbyn

THE FIVE SINS

Deceit

Distortion

Personal gain

Failures of leadership

Gloating, hubris and frivolity

CONTENTS

The Warning from Cato the Younger   1

The Beach at Dunkirk: The Beach at Kos   7

From the Sick Man of Europe to the World's Fifth
    Strongest Economy and its Top Soft Power, 1973–2016   15

Towards the Edge of a Precipice   29

World Wars I and II: The Genesis, 1915–1955   41

Britain's Late and Mangled Joining, 1955–1975   51

The Emergence of the Single Currency, 1979–1992   63

The Twilight Years of Thatcher, 1990–2013   69

John Major's Bastards, 1990–1997   79

Baloney and Bananas, 1990–2015   89

Blair Ducks the Advocacy, 1997–2007   99

Blinkered Brussels, 1985–2015   107

Tory Implosion, 1997–2010   117

The Rise of Nationalistic Populism, 2005–2016   127

Multiple Referendum Errors, 2013–2016   135

The Foaming of the Press Barons, 2015–2016   145

Campaign Follies, February–June 2016   155

Campaign Deceits and Distortions, 2015–2016   165

Crapulent Corbyn and the Implosion of Labour, 2015–2016   177

Berlin, Brussels, and Paris: Failure of Imagination, 2015–2016   187

Envoi   195

Chronology   197

Appendix: The Warning from Cato the Younger   204

'Very well, alone'
– DAVID LOW, 18 JUNE 1940

Cartoon by David Low / Solo Syndication

CHAPTER I

THE WARNING FROM
CATO THE YOUNGER

SEVENTY-SEVEN YEARS AGO, my great-grandfather, 'Cato', wrote a book published in July 1940, castigating fifteen politicians and officials, the 'Men of Munich', for failing to prepare Britain sufficiently in the 1930s to face Hitler's militaristic Germany.

The book had an enormous impact, shredding the reputations of two Conservative Prime Ministers, Stanley Baldwin and Neville Chamberlain, while ignoring one of the greatest appeasers Max Beaverbrook, who was subsidising anti-war candidates until early 1940, and who was the patron of its principal author, Michael Foot. The issues were nevertheless more clear-cut than today. The evils of Nazi Germany were plain for all to see, and it was easy, indeed simplistic, for Cato to attack his targets, many of whom were scapegoats for a series of decisions over which they had little freedom of manoeuvre, and which appeared less foolish over time. But Britain needed figures to blame during the war, and so long as the final outcome was in the balance, castigating these figures served a cathartic purpose.

The guilty men charge some seventy years later is subtler. Beyond doubt is that that there has been folly, distortion, deceit and failure of leadership throughout the whole sad saga of Britain's membership of the EU. So, it is again a family duty to take up the pen to warn against error and to highlight the mistakes that have been made, in the hope that in the coming months and years, wiser counsels may prevail.

Britain is to leave the European Union, the alliance which it joined in January 1973. This is a very big decision. Andrew Marr described it as Britain's 'single biggest democratic vote ... ever'. The book does not point the finger of blame at all those who strove for Britain's departure from the EU. Good men and women, and compelling arguments, were to be found on both sides of the longest debate in modern British history. Rather, it highlights just fifteen, deemed to be guilty of one or more of these sins, some more serious than others. Anger is common in many of those most passionate about Brexit, and a nastiness, a hatred indeed can be found in many of the most ardent too.

1. Deceit
2. Distortion
3. Placing personal gain above duty
4. Failures of leadership
5. Gloating, hubris and frivolity

The quality of debate on the value of Britain to the EU has been remarkably poor over the past thirty years. From the 1990s onwards, most of the British press lost no opportunity to disparage the EU, justifying themselves on the grounds that it was what their readers wanted to hear. In the face of almost uniform press hostility, successive political leaders failed to stand up and make a positive and responsible case for Britain in Europe.

The fact that politicians have always scaremongered, none worse than Churchill in the 1945 general election, and the press have distorted the truth, cannot be used as an excuse or to legitimise what happened during the long EU referendum.

Leaders in Europe are to blame too. They have often been too poor in quality, insufficient to the task of defining a role for those nations which never wanted to be at the heart of the EU, but who wanted to be a part of the EU. Where were the visionary figures of the calibre of the EU's founding fathers, Jean

Monnet and Konrad Adenauer? Such were needed to devise a new architecture for the EU, but were not to be found when most needed. The EU instead became clogged by second-rate functionaries and bureaucrats, when it needed people with imagination and intelligence.

With almost no national leader or press outlet in the UK actively speaking for Britain's membership, and with dullards running the EU, all it needed for a perfect Brexit storm was for three factors to coincide. It came with a short-term crisis that threatened British livelihoods and values, a demagogue able to galvanise populist fervour, and a series of events that would trigger the calling of a referendum. There was nothing inevitable about Britain leaving the EU.

Cato had an easier task in 1940 because he could argue that the policy of appeasement pursued during the 1930s had been an abject failure. War *had* come: Britain *was* underprepared for it. There is no such clear Brexit disaster. Indeed, the year following the referendum has not seen the dire consequences that the Remainers augured. It is inevitable, however, that if and when the downsides of British departure begin seriously to materialise, the hardened high-priests of Brexit will seek to blame Remain figures in the UK and abroad for negative results. They will never question their own actions, or admit personal responsibility. They are the guiltiest of all. Already, strident Brexit commentators are redefining the entire argument on their own terms. My warning is timely.

It is not too late for Britain to find a more intelligent way forward. The EU sooner or later will have to fundamentally reform itself. Had the referendum decision been to remain in the EU, Britain could have shaped the reformulation of the EU from the inside. As it is, Britain will have to stand impotently aside while others wrench the EU back from a European superstate project towards the ideals of unity and diversity, which reached a high point in its early years.

Guilty Men: The Brexit Edition will be dismissed by some as a moaner's manual, such is the polarised nature of the contemporary debate. The authors, however, are no romantic Remoaners: they ardently wish Britain to flourish and be stronger outside the EU, and for the twenty-first century to be a period of unparalleled prosperity, peace and tolerance across Britain and Europe. Britain must find a way of remaining as close as possible to the EU in all areas where the gains palpably outweigh the disadvantages and the risks.

The guilty men of 1940 were reprieved by the decisive leadership of key figures over the following five years. Expiation is always at hand.

CHAPTER II

THE BEACH AT DUNKIRK:
THE BEACH AT KOS

A blazing, ferocious sun beats down on a beach which offers no shade; none except for the few precious square inches beneath the lighthouse and the pier. The sea runs out shallow for many yards from the sand and beyond the beach; between it and the town the sand dunes rise, providing at least some pretence of cover. Mark well the dunes, the shallow sea and, most of all, the pier. The lives of three hundred thousand troops were to depend on those accidental amenities.

CATO'S 1940 *GUILTY MEN* begins with this evocation of the beaches of Dunkirk. Because it is in a book about war, one reads an ominous undertone in what might otherwise – apart from the literary flourish and the last sentence – be from a holiday brochure. An old Europe died on those beaches. Fortunately, the terrifying New Order that replaced it was short-lived, although the Germans held out to the end in the fortress of Dunkirk before surrendering to the combined Czechoslovak, Canadian, Scottish and French forces that had besieged the occupied port.

British historical memory has transmuted the 1940 evacuation from Dunkirk into some sort of victory. The operation itself was a triumph of courage, improvisation and defiance. To Cato: 'That night a miracle was born. This land of Britain is rich in heroes. She had brave, daring men in her Navy and Air Force as well as in her Army. She had heroes in jerseys and sweaters and old rubber boots in all the fishing ports of Britain.'

But Dunkirk need never have happened. As Cato wrote, albeit simplistically, the chain of events that led to Dunkirk was a saga of blunders, missed opportunities, imperfect politicians, and an electorate that responded to Baldwin's promise that 'there will be no great armaments' in 1935 by giving him a landslide. Europe's darkest hour followed Dunkirk. The failure in the West meant that when the Nazi tide was rolled back, the Soviet Union – whose oil had fuelled the Nazi planes that filled the skies over Dunkirk – would extend its control deep into central Europe and the Iron Curtain would split our European home into two blocs.

The Dunkirk myth helped in the short term; it and Church-ill's magnificent belligerence stiffened British resistance and maybe even saved European civilisation. 'Very well, alone,' as David Low's evocative cartoon at the front of this book put it on 18 June 1940.

The Dunkirk spirit was an effective medicinal blend in 1940, but at difficult intervals in peacetime, British politicians and the media have swigged from the bottle of an inferior blend which seems to be mixed with toxic, blindness-inducing in-gredients. The call for a retreat from Europe in 2016 – and the harsh, ugly mood that set in before and afterwards – was fuelled by long abuse of the Dunkirk spirit, particularly by the British press which was inclined to xenophobic ranting under its intoxicating influence.

'Very well, alone' has been darkly misrepresented as a defi-ant expression of Britain's default approach to the rest of the world. It lies behind the thinking of many Brexiteers. Britain was greatest in its history when it stood alone. Britain can stand alone again outside Europe if it is to be great again. Yet in 1940 it was a desperate last resort. Two days before Low's cartoon, Churchill had proposed to French Prime Minister Paul Rey-naud that Britain and France should become an 'indissoluble' (not just 'ever closer') political union with common foreign, economic and defence policies and a formal association between the two parliaments. True, it was another desperate throw to keep France in the war rather than a well-considered plan, but on the morrow of Dunkirk a radical sort of political union was considered preferable to going it alone.

But it is a myth that Britain stood alone. It was not alone, even in June 1940. Britain was supported by the Commonwealth (and the Empire, in its un-free way) in its resistance to the Nazis, and London was host to a mini European Union of governments in exile. Brave Poles, Czechs and Slovaks fought on from Britain and served with honour in the Battle of Britain and the siege of Dunkirk. While France collapsed, General de Gaulle escaped to carry on the fight and deliver his inspired Appeal of 18 June, a text that the British should celebrate alongside Churchill's oratory.

Post-war both Churchill and de Gaulle had complex, ambivalent feelings about nationalism and European unity, struggling with the prospect of the decline of their two empires, the need to ensure peace in Europe and the extent to which Britain should be part of the project. There was a balance to be struck between union and the proud states of France and the United Kingdom, and it was not easy. Their legacy is degraded and dishonoured by the current generation of their would-be successors, ultra-nationalists including Marine Le Pen and Nigel Farage and their camp followers in the press.

The politicians of the post-war era created a careful balance, a delicate web of connections based not on secret diplomatic pacts or selfish nationalism, but on the strong bonds of peace, trade and cultural exchange.

Seventy-five years on, most of Europe, including Britain, had forgotten the agony of being at war. A continent long (and mostly) at peace, rising incomes and the boom of aviation had made the islands of Greece places where Europe's modestly affluent could lie on beaches under the warm Mediterranean sun. The peoples of the West felt entitled to a moment where they could forget their concerns and relax. Never mind the economic collapse of Greece – a product of a corrupt and incompetent set of Greek governments and Europe's conniv-ance with them in the interests of political and economic unity. The sun shone, bodies bronzed.

But in 2015, European beaches became once again a place of desperation, as people arrived again in an armada of little boats from the war zones of Syria and Iraq and squalid camps along the eastern Mediterranean.

The mass population movements caused by the wars in Syria and Libya and the inhuman behaviour of both the Assad regime and ISIS posed profound moral questions. We can debate whether the root cause of the migration could have been better dealt with by military action or diplomacy or both, and whether there were ways of responding to the humanitarian disaster without inadvertently helping criminal traffickers. Germany opened its doors; in Britain there was a moment of solidarity at the sad sight of little Alan Kurdi, washed up dead on the beach in September 2015. But it was short lived. Britain put up the shutters as far as it could, even passing but then failing to implement the 'Dubs amendment' to permit the entry of unaccompanied refugee children.

Cameron's government did at least use British aid intelligently in supporting Syrian refugees in the camps of Jordan and Lebanon, where the refugee crisis was beyond the imagination of most of Western Europe. Many volunteers from Britain and other countries did heroic work in the Greek islands. But there were also holidaymakers who whinged that reality had intruded into their idyll. One such, in Kos, was rebuked by an elderly fish seller on the harbour side in the presence of a *Guardian* reporter: 'Lady, you'd rather have bodies on the beaches? Tsk. We knew war here too once,' he said, fixing her with a beady eye.

Callous indifference was preferable to the response of some, who wanted the men, women and children in the boats to be drowned. At its grossest, a columnist in Britain's bestselling newspaper, *The Sun*, drew on Nazi and Rwandan genocidal propaganda to proclaim that 'these migrants are cockroaches'.

The scenes on the beaches of Kos, and the primal fears of being overrun by hordes from the uncivilised side of the Channel (or the Mediterranean) were not forgotten by some of the most unscrupulous campaigners in British politics. A year later, on the day Jo Cox, a pro-Europe, pro-refugee rights politician, was assassinated on 16 June 2016 by a fascist, Nigel Farage unveiled his 'Breaking Point' poster. It portrayed a defiant Farage centre shot, and behind him a long, winding column of desperate humanity, under the bold title 'Breaking Point. The EU has failed us all. We must break free of the EU and take back control of our borders.'

The more subtle, house-trained exploiters of fear and xenophobia in the official Leave campaign made much the same point by inference, with a menacing map of 'countries set to join the EU' (a misleading term in itself) which to the casual reader (and what other sort of reader of political leaflets is there?) looked as if they might include Syria and Iraq. Vote Leave or the barbarian hordes will be next washing up on our beaches in Kent, Essex and Sussex in their flotilla of little ships.

The poster and leaflet carry a faint, degraded echo of 'Very well, alone'. But it is in the 1930s spirit of appeasement, callousness self-pity and defeat rather than the true Dunkirk spirit.

Britain throughout its history has been at its best when it has been high-minded, progressive, patriotic, interconnected with the rest of the world and generous. That is the true Dunkirk spirit. Not mean-minded, xenophobic, racist and ideologically nationalistic.

How on earth did we get here?

CHAPTER III

FROM THE SICK MAN OF EUROPE TO THE WORLD'S FIFTH STRONGEST ECONOMY AND ITS TOP SOFT POWER, 1973–2016

THE IDEA THAT BRITAIN would be much stronger without the EU was one of the hallmarks of the Leave campaign. We cannot let this assertion be unexamined, not least because those fighting for Remain made such a feeble case for the benefits of EU membership during the campaign. Britain's economic strength was referenced by Leave not as a reason to remain in the Union, but as a motivation to leave. Against all those who argued Britain would be weakened without membership, the reply came that, as arch-Brexiteer and MEP Daniel Hannan put it, 'Britain is the fifth largest economy in the world, the fourth military power, a leading member of the G7 and one of five permanent seat-holders on the UN Security

Council. I think we might just about scrape by.' Very well, alone, indeed.

But more than that, the EU was actively blamed for holding Britain back. Lead Brexit politician Boris Johnson lambasted the EU as 'a job-destroyer engine, you can see it all across southern Europe and you can see it alas in this country as well'. If we left, veteran Eurosceptic John Redwood argued, 'the economy would get a boost, our public services would be better funded, and some hated taxes could be removed'. Michael Gove, a pivotal figure in the Brexit campaign, claimed 'the majority of people in this country are suffering as a result of our membership of the European Union'. Leaving the EU thus became, in Nigel Farage's words, 'the logical, practical and safe thing to do'. Safer and stronger.

How easy to forget that back in the 1970s, prior to membership of the European Union, Britain was known as the sick man of Europe. 'It isn't easy today to recall quite how much British politicians accepted the inevitability of national decline in the 1960s and 1970s,' writes historian Andrew Roberts. 'Militant trade unionism, falling productivity, sterling crises, oil-price hikes, stock market crashes: it was a dangerous and depressing time for Britain.' No surprise then that Britain tried twice to join the EU's forerunner, the European Economic Community (EEC), in the 1960s before eventually joining in January 1973, when Britain was firmly on the slide. Closer alignment with Europe was embarked upon as a way of slowing and perhaps reversing that decline. In the twenty-five years since the end of the Second World War, Labour and Conservative governments had, despite repeated attempts at political, economic and cultural renewal, failed to find the dynamism necessary to acquire a settled and confident place in the post war world. Not since the loss of the American colonies in the 1780s had British morale been at such a low.

By 2016, however, Britain had changed from the sick man of Europe, the 'dangerous and depressing place' in Roberts's words, to a powerhouse in the world, a major financial, cultural and political presence with the fifth largest economy based on GDP, having overtaken France in 2014. Britain had become a significant player not only in Europe, but also on the world stage: a powerful figure in the Group of Seven, retaining its seat on the UN Security Council, consistently the closest country to the United States, and an increasingly close friend to China and India. The British language, culture, creative industries and traditions were respected across the world. No longer was Britain laughed and sneered at as it had been in the early 1970s.

We will never know how much of this transformation was due to Britain's membership of the EU. Perhaps Britain might have performed even better outside the EU, though its trajectory until 1973 suggests that might have been unlikely. But no one can fairly assert that membership of the EU *prevented* this. Not even those who believe every improvement to Britain is owed to Margaret Thatcher's liberalisations in the 1980s. The EU no more prevented her work than it could prevent the achievement of any determined Prime Minister. The EU's influence over government policy has been greatly exaggerated.

The economic transformation in Britain was skewed towards London and the south-east with a few bright spots across the rest of the country, including Manchester, Birmingham, Glasgow and Edinburgh. Many across Britain have felt left behind over the last forty years. The better the national economy and the south-east performed, the more the imbalance caused offence. No surprise then that the 'left-behind' areas voted overwhelmingly against Britain's continuing in the EU. But it is hard to maintain that their relative disadvantage was *because of* Britain's membership. More likely, the contrasts would have been even more marked had Britain not been a member and it is indeed these very areas that, on some projections, will be the ones who are hardest hit after Britain exits the EU.

ECONOMY AND TRADE

Unlike its neighbours in Western Europe, Britain emerged

from the Second World War unambiguously victorious. Initially, this was reflected in the strength of its economy. GDP per capita in the UK was some 90 per cent bigger than the average of the six founding members of the EU (Belgium, France, Germany, Italy, Luxembourg and the Netherlands) in 1945. This relative strength fortified the British Labour government in declining the Schuman Plan's European Coal and Steel Community (ECSC) in 1950. Although the Continental countries were beginning to recover, the UK's per capita GDP was still a third larger in 1955.

By the late 1960s, however, following a decade of integration for the EU6, France, West Germany and Italy – the three founder members of the EEC closest in size to the UK – were producing more per person than Britain. By 1973, the year Britain joined, their average GDP per head almost doubled, rising by 95 per cent. Meanwhile GDP in Britain rose by only 50 per cent over the same period: it was now 7 per cent smaller than the EU6 average.

Membership coincided with the end of Britain's relative economic decline and since then, Britain's GDP has grown faster than that of other EU countries; only Germany remains ahead of it in Europe as a world economic power (behind the US, China and Japan). The nature of the British economy has also been changed: in 1948, 46 per cent of GDP came from the service sector and by 2013 this number had reached 79 per cent. The EU has played a pivotal role in this, with member states now accounting for 44 per cent of all UK exports in goods and services, £240 billion out of the £550 billion (27 per cent of GDP) total that exports collectively contribute. Did Brexiteers overlook the significance of Britain's active role in the European Union's single market: a fifth of the global economy in itself?

Crucially, these benefits have not been siphoned off just to a southern elite. Poorer regions of the UK are more dependent on exports to the EU than richer ones: a significant percentage of private sector output in the north-east of England, one of Britain's poorest regions and who voted most consistently in favour of Leave, consists of EU exports, far higher than other regions. Similarly, Wales and Northern Ireland, two of the most deprived regions of Britain, are net beneficiaries of the EU Budget, in the form of agricultural subsidies and regional development funds. The north-east and North Yorkshire are also set to lose £665 million of EU funding after 2020. The EU has been a key ingredient in Britain's economic strength. Avoiding entrenching Britain's regional inequality after leaving may not be the 'oh, I think we'll scrape by' breeze that was promised to those areas.

FINANCE

In the 1960s, the City of London's stature was as an international clearing centre for exclusively sterling-based transactions. Now, it is one of the leading finance centres in the world, dealing in multiple currencies and providing the full range of international financial services. In 2016, it provided over two million jobs, 7.3 per cent of the UK's total, and contributed £124 billion in gross value added. Its trade surplus of approximately £72 billion is greater than that of all other exporting sectors combined.

Whatever the reputation of bankers, then, the significance of financial services to the British economy cannot be denied. But nor can the role of the EU in the financial industry's success. Over the years, its transactions have also become increasingly tilted towards the Eurozone. Financial services and insurance make up the largest proportion of the UK's services trade, accounting for £22.7 billion (26 per cent) of services exports to the EU.

In 1997, other EU member states accounted for 30 per cent of the accumulated stock of foreign direct investment (FDI) in Britain; by 2012, this proportion had risen to 50 per cent. In 2013, no fewer than two thirds of EU financial services were handled by the City, while EU banks held £1.4 trillion of assets in London, about 17 per cent of the country's total bank assets, far exceeding those held from the US. To the benefit of Britain, then, the City has emerged not only as the largest global financial centre in the EU, but also as the centre of the Eurozone's financial system itself. How will leaving the EU enhance that role, on which Britain's economic vitality hinges?

CREATIVE INDUSTRIES

The UK's creative industries, which include IT, television, film and music, are worth £87.4 billion to the UK economy, with the number rising each year at a faster pace than the UK economy as a whole. In 2016 the creative economy accounted for 2.9 million jobs, 9 per cent of all jobs in the UK. The value of services exported by the UK Creative Industries in 2014 (when the latest set of figures is available) was £19.8 billion, up 10 per cent from the year before. Over half of these exports, 57.3 per cent, were sent to Europe, generating £11.4 billion in revenue. The US was the next largest recipient, taking 25.3 per cent of the total exports, generating £5 billion.

Over the years since entry to the EU, Britain has created dynamic creative industries that lead Europe. The UK now has the largest games development sector in Europe, generating £2 billion in global sales each year and contributing some £1 billion to national GDP. London, meanwhile, is widely considered to be the digital capital of Europe, with part of east London, 'Tech City', home to hundreds of digital, high-tech firms.

Again, it is impossible to say whether this transformation has happened because, or despite, of Britain's EU membership, but we can say with certainty that the EU hasn't stopped it. The EU is certainly not the 'job-destroyer' Brexiteers like Johnson claimed it to be. Moreover, the EU has helped cement English as the *lingua franca* across all of Europe – even former Soviet states. English is crucial to the creative industries.

The creative industries have become a cornerstone of Britain's 'soft power' as well. Institutions like the BBC, the British Museum and the Royal Shakespeare Company are recognised as world leaders in their fields and act as key cultural exports. The 'Soft Power 30 Index', which ranks countries using extensive data, placed the UK first, ahead of Germany, the US and France: its report identified the prestige and success of Britain's creative industries as key.

The irony is that the Brexit proponents of 'Great Britain' have jeopardised this greatness. How can Britain be higher than first?

UNIVERSITIES AND SCHOOLS

The university and school sector before British entry was

languishing. In 1973, British universities were predominantly inward-looking and disconnected from their local communities, enterprise, and the corporate sector. Now there are university parks everywhere and the university sector plays a dynamic part in the economy. According to the *Times Higher Education* ranking, three British Universities – Oxford, Cambridge and Imperial – are ranked among the ten best in the world, while another four make the top forty. But the transformational story is in the large number of lesser-known British universities which have scaled up the world rankings since 1973. Yes, all this might have happened outside the EU. But the trajectory has been impressive within the EU.

This rising global stature has been mirrored by an increasingly internationalist element in its research. Almost all the growth in UK output is in the form of international collaborations. In science, the prevalence of research papers co-authored by researchers from more than one country has risen sharply. Since 1981, the number of academic papers written by international authors in the UK has risen from 15 per cent to over 50 per cent today. Of the UK's international collaborations, 80 per cent include an EU partner. Collectively, the EU remains the world leader in terms of its global share of science researchers (22.2 per cent), ahead of China (19.1 per cent) and the US (16.7 per cent), according to a recent UNESCO science report.

Schools, meanwhile, have been partly transformed. In 1973, they were often dull and regimented. Our comprehensive schools were the norm across the state sector at secondary level, while the independent sector kept itself almost totally apart, run on fundamentally the same principles as before the Second World War. By 2016, academies, free schools and academy chains had introduced a fresh, if uneven, dynamism into the state sector, while the independent sector had reinvented itself as offering some of the most dynamic schools in the world, which aspiring families from across the world sought to send their children. The continuing and deadening presence of dull uniformity and state-imposed examination and curriculum came not from Europe, but was imposed by Whitehall and Westminster. The most dynamic curriculum in British schools unsurprisingly was not a home-grown product, but rather the International Baccalaureate which is widely followed in Europe, and which would have grown far more quickly across state schools had it been supported by central government.

A TOLERANT SOCIETY

The staid, patriarchal and establishment-heavy society that permeated Britain in the first twenty years after the war, began to change at the very moment Britain applied to join the EEC. The

first Wilson government (1964–70) inspired by Roy Jenkins, the
modernising Home Secretary (1965–67), introduced a range of
social reforms including the effective abolition of capital punishment, the partial decriminalisation of homosexuality and the
relaxing of divorce and abortion law. After entry to the EU came
the Sex Discrimination Act in 1975 and the Race Relations Act
in 1976, and later on the equalisation of age consent with the
Sexual Offences (Amendment) Bill in 2000, the creation of the
public sector 'Equality Duty' (2010) and the introduction of
gay marriage in 2013. Europe, above all, through the European
Court of Human Rights (though not part of the EU), was responsible for pushing the British government to liberalise the
rights of the LGBT community. Without doubt, excessive immigration threatened the equilibrium in some areas. But Britain
by 2016 was one of the most liberal and tolerant countries on
earth, and multi-ethnic London, the capital of the world. The
young overwhelmingly liked the benefits the EU brought, and
voted over 70 per cent to remain. Many worry about what Brexit
will bring.

A GOLDEN ERA

Britain indeed experienced a 'golden era' between 1973 and
2016, during which education, healthcare, material living, the
environment and well-being improved immeasurably. Britain

became a dynamic presence on the world stage, confident and proud. People were no longer surprised that Britain came second in the Olympic Games in 2016, behind only the US. Such success was taken almost for granted. In 1972, 'dangerous and depressing' Britain had come twelfth.

We risk losing all of this. Britain may thrive. But we may find ourselves isolated, friendless, economically challenged, unable to meet our commitments, forced to tax the elderly and the infirm, while demanding young people pick up the tab.

CHAPTER IV

TOWARDS THE EDGE
OF A PRECIPICE

NO ONE KNOWS HOW Brexit will turn out for Britain. Perhaps the wonderful benefits that leavers have told us about will shower down upon the length and breadth of a glorious, newly energised and 'liberated' country. We have had promises aplenty: 'Let's give our NHS the £350 million the EU takes every week. That's enough to build a new NHS hospital every week of the year', 'taking control' of immigration and relieving the 'big strain' on the NHS, 'higher wages for working people outside the EU ... because pay will no longer be undercut by uncontrolled migration', 'increased funding to science' while 'still saving billions'. Independent 'very well, alone' Britain might flow with milk and honey, with union jacks and the singing of 'Rule Britannia'.

But perhaps some of the claims and warnings made by Remainers during the referendum campaign, often hyperbolic

and negative, will come to pass. We can be certain that if they
do, the Brexit camp will place the blame on anyone but themselves. The guilty men will be absent at the reckoning. Like
Macavity, the Mystery Cat, they will not be there. Why, then,
has this book not waited for publication until the downsides
manifested themselves? After all, in 1940, the abject failure of
the policy of appeasement was demonstrably clear to all. The
case for publishing now is because Brexit is by any measure
a risk, because leavers deliberately obfuscated and played
the risks down, and because an awareness of those risks will
help our leaders shape Britain's policy more wisely if taken
fully into account. What then, might these risks be? Some
have been visited already, but bear restating briefly.

TRADE AND ECONOMIC

Forty-five per cent of Britain's trade of goods and services is
with the EU, the largest market. In terms of goods and services, an authoritative estimate by the Institute for Fiscal Studies
(IFS) is that within ten years of Brexit taking place there will
be a comparative loss of anywhere between 3 and 7 per cent
of GDP. But even if the figure proves an overestimate, why
have we risked a loss of this kind of magnitude? Much will
depend upon the deal that Britain manages to reach with the

EU, as well as with other trading nations including India and China. At present, some Brexiteers operate with an 'imperial reflex' mentality, believing that other countries are charitable institutions who are there to help Britain. Perhaps favourable agreements will be reached: but what if they are not? Many foreign companies, including car manufacturers, American investment banks and business service corporations moved their offices to the UK to access the EU market. It is hard to see why foreign investment into the UK might rise. Automobile and aerospace companies depend on integrated supply chains, which means that retailers will face increasing difficulties. Why risk the loss to trade, to investment, to productivity growth? Why put at risk Britain's ability to attract and retain the best talent, at a time when dynamic and creative people are much needed?

LOSS OF INFLUENCE OVER EU POLICY

The EU, Britain's largest trading partner, makes decisions on a wide variety of policy areas, including trade and transport. After Brexit, these decisions will be taken by EU governments and Britain will have no influence other than as a lobbyist. As a large member state, Britain has had weighted votes in the council, votes in the European Parliament, and has been active in lobbying in Brussels. The 2008 financial crisis provided a key instance of when this British influence was exercised. Mario Monti, European Commissioner for Competition, came to London to listen and learn, and the action plan he took back to Europe was heavily influenced by Britain. The country will no longer have this opportunity for leverage, nor will it be able to take part in free trade agreements between the EU and the rest of the world. Without British influence, the EU may become a less economically liberal and more centralised economy. Or a 'two-speed' Europe might emerge, with an inner and outer tier. Britain will continue to trade with the EU, and will be eager not to break itself off entirely from its deliberations. But it would be folly to imagine that Britain's voice will be heard, above all in those areas that are most in Britain's interests but not in the rest of the European Union's.

THE CITY OF LONDON

The City, we are told, will flourish in the newly liberated climate of post-Brexit Britain. Chunks of the City will, however, move elsewhere: to Brussels, Frankfurt or New York. The City of London is a dynamic place that has weathered ups and downs in the past. It will certainly survive, but will it ever again recover the position that it enjoyed before Brexit?

FOREIGN, DEFENCE AND SECURITY POLICY

Once Britain leaves the EU, it must find a fresh role for itself. In the post-war era before Britain joined the EU, the Commonwealth and British Empire counted for something. No more. Dean Acheson, the former US Secretary of State, said in 1962, 'Britain has lost an empire and has not yet found a role.' Finding the role may not be so easy and Britain may find the elevated status it enjoyed on the global stage in 2016 diminished once it is outside. Decisions will be taken at the EU Council, where Britain will no longer be present. Yet many of Britain's foreign policy interests and values are shared with the EU, including the Iran nuclear deal, peace in the Balkans, standing up to Russia, working out a common line on economic trade deals with China, and keeping the United Nations strong. Without a share in the EU voice, which so amplified Britain's own, it may become a weaker voice in the world. Britain's importance may diminish in the eyes of India and China. A fear on entering the EEC was that Britain's relationship with the US would be weakened after entry: in fact, the opposite happened. Forty-three years of membership saw the relationship reach the highest levels of intimacy in peacetime history. Since 1973 successive White House administrations have viewed Britain as a way into the EU. In the future, US

Presidents, differences of language notwithstanding, may well focus more on the French and Germans and steer away from Britain.

THE EU MAY LOSE WITHOUT BRITAIN

The departure of Britain may prove to be the catalyst for profound and long overdue fundamental reform of the EU. The victory of Emmanuel Macron in the French presidential election in May 2017, succeeding the feeble François Hollande, may well provide the figure who can help shape that reform process. The loss of Britain unbalances the European Union. It was set up in the 1950s partly to contain German power: fears will grow, not least in France and Italy, that German power cannot be shackled without Britain's presence. If the EU begins to unravel, if nationalistic voices strengthen again, as seen in Germany, Austria, France and Holland, who is to say that Europe in the twenty-first century will not descend again into war, which blighted so many previous centuries, but has been absent since the creation of the EU? The EU has proved a potent support to peace, democracy and the rule of law across greater Europe. What might replace it?

UNITY OF THE UNITED KINGDOM

The result of the EU referendum did not provide the

short-term impetus which Nicola Sturgeon and her Scottish National Party (SNP) had hoped for. The imminent departure of Britain from the EU has not provided the springboard for Remain-voting Scotland to have a second referendum, which, unlike the 55:45 per cent Scottish referendum result on 18 September 2014, might provide a 'yes' vote. The immediate opportunity, or danger, of a second referendum is past. But who is to say that Britain's exit from the EU will not eventually provide the pretext for a second referendum on Scottish Independence, as well as additional ammunition for a Leave vote, especially if the Scottish economy deteriorates outside the EU? Ireland is a further concern, as the delicate peace process may be put at risk. It is not fanciful to imagine that the decision could destabilise the fragile peace in Northern Ireland, or a reunification of Ireland after a hundred years. Scottish independence and the return of the Troubles to Northern Ireland may thus both have been brought closer by the vote for Brexit. Why have the progress and achievement of so many years of hard work been jeopardised? But, as Brexiteers told us in 2016, such talk was just scaremongering.

UNIVERSITIES AND SCIENCE

Britain's impending exit from the EU creates real uncertainty for British higher education. Theresa May has refused to reveal her hand before the negotiations, or to confirm the rights of EU higher education staff to remain and work in the UK post-Brexit. This uncertainty risks a 'brain drain' of the most able academics and deters academics from other countries coming in the first place, compounded by the loss of funding from the EU. According to the Office for National Statistics (ONS), between 2007 and 2013, the UK contributed €5.4 billion to the EU for research, development and innovation, receiving €8.8 billion in return. Without EU funding, UK universities might have struggled to earn their global reputation. British universities could yet flourish outside the EU, as others do in Israel, Norway and Switzerland. But it will require a step change in thinking.

Currently, the government includes overseas students in its net migration target, which it aims to reduce to below 100,000 a year. A Select Committee report advised the government against such controls, warning they threaten the UK's share of the international student market. EU students generated an estimated £3.7 billion for the UK economy and 34,000 jobs in 2011/12. The government needs to find a way of continuing its appeal to EU students, not only for economic reasons, but to preserve the diversity of the student body. In February 2017, UCAS recorded a drop of 7 per cent in EU students applying to study in the UK in February 2017. This does not bode well.

British science was at a high in 2016. International, especially EU, cooperation has been vital to its success. Research may well be damaged by Brexit. Many jobs hinge on this. President of the Royal Society, Lord Rees, worries that Brexit could do 'irreversible' damage to both 'big' and 'small' science, which have flourished since Britain joined the EU.

CREATIVE INDUSTRIES

As a world leader in the creative industries, Britain attracts the best talent from all over the world. Incoming talent has been crucial in addressing creative skills gaps in the workforce, due to the longstanding marginalisation of creative education in the UK. The UK has benefited enormously from EU funding; from Creative Europe for cultural and audio-visual projects; to the European Regional Development Fund (ERDF), which has contributed towards vital regional infrastructure; to funding through innovation programme Horizon 2020. It has been confirmed that Britain will lose its access to ERDF, with the status of Horizon 2020 and Creative Europe funding remaining uncertain.

Without freedom of movement in the EU, artists may face bureaucratic and financial barriers. Visas may become a necessity, which would create serious problems for performing arts companies, as many rely on international touring for their livelihoods – which accounts for more than half of their revenue in many cases. If this kind of touring is not sustainable, the whole company could fold. The progress of the creative industries, the fastest growing sector of the UK economy since the 2008 financial crash, could be jeopardised.

The creative industries currently count for over 10 per cent of UK service exports, with over half of these going to Europe. Without a good trade deal, this would be lost.

TOLERANCE

Within the EU, Britain became a more open, tolerant, diverse and inclusive society. London, despite Brexit, may well remain one of the most globalised and tolerant cities in the world. But the rest of the country? Many of those who voted against the EU did so because they want a closed, not an open Britain. They vex about globalisation, foreign investment, immigrants. They are nativists. How ironic if those who campaigned for a more open, global Britain, achieve the opposite?

Let us hope that Britain flourishes outside the EU. Let us hope that none of the risks raised in this chapter come to transpire. Let us indeed hope that the fears and concerns of the Remainers prove to be without substance, and that only good will flow. But all these risks are real, present and serious.

One of the risks too is that the EU will at last reform itself in Britain's absence, and that the EU will re-emerge as the strong player that it was in its first two decades, and become a major economic and political power in the world – a power from which Britain, to its detriment, is excluded.

Britain stands on the edge. Were the arguments in favour of Brexit sound and certain enough to justify the risk we are taking?

Perhaps, just perhaps, both sides of the debate have been too histrionic. Perhaps the membership of the EU is not the seismic event, for good or bad, that it has been made out to be. Why, then, take the risk?

CHAPTER V

WORLD WARS I AND II: THE GENESIS, 1915-1955

THE EU WAS ALWAYS more than an economic union. A political dimension was explicit from the moment it was founded in 1957. It was born out of war and conceived as a way of finding a better future for Europe than fighting. An understanding of history, so absent from the debates over the EU on both sides, is now required. For almost a hundred years after the Battle of Waterloo in June 1815, Europe had been largely at peace, but in the summer of 1914, its leaders rushed headlong, or sleepwalked, into the Great War.

On 14 June 1915, Second Lieutenant Douglas Gillespie wrote a letter from the trenches to his former headmaster at Winchester College, Montague Rendall. Gillespie's brother, Tom, who had taken part in the 1912 Olympics, had been killed near to where he was fighting. His mind turned to the end of the war and how a better world might emerge from all the suffering. The idea was born in his mind of a tree-shaded *Via Sacra* running between the trench lines from Switzerland to the English Channel. 'I would like every man, woman and child in Western Europe to go on pilgrimage along that *Via Sacra*,' he wrote of his imaginary 450-mile European memorial, 'so that they might think and learn what it all means from the silent witness of either side'. Gillespie did not live to discover that his proposal had gone the same way as so many of those fine ideals conceived during the war. He was killed in action at the Battle of Loos on 25 September 1915.

By the time the war eventually ground to a halt in November 1918, there were 38 million casualties, including 17 million dead (of whom some 7 million were civilians). While the fighting was still in progress, the hope grew that this was 'the war to end war'. The term was first coined by H. G. Wells, who blamed Germany and her allies for the outbreak of hostilities, and believed that only the defeat of German militarism would bring an end to war. In subsequent years, the phrase became associated with US President Woodrow Wilson though he is believed to have only used it once.

The economic depression from 1929 finally killed off hopes of a more peaceful Europe after the First World War. In 1930, Winston Churchill, a master of ambiguity on the topic of European unification, argued that 'the conception of a United

States of Europe is right'. He saw earlier than many that the Treaty of Versailles of 1919 would be incapable of producing a lasting settlement of the deep and raw divisions between France and Germany. 'Every step taken' to end the enmity between these nations, he wrote, 'which appeases the obsolete hatreds and vanished oppressions which makes easier the traffic in reciprocal services of Europe, which encourages nations to lay aside their precautionary panoply, is good in itself.'

Gillespie's dream of a *Via Sacra* faded quickly. In the 1920s, the trenches and battlefields were ploughed over by farmers and returned to agriculture. Before long, people forgot what the war was for, and what lessons might be learnt. But if there was one lesson from the First World War, and the killing and maiming of millions, it is that war rarely resolves anything. In the case of the First World War, Europe learnt nothing. Interwar attempts at reinforcing peace often amounted to little more than unenforceable words and blind hope in the League of Nations. Nationalism, demagoguery and xenophobia were rife. From the early 1930s, peace was challenged by nationalists who either overtly believed that might made right, or made bilateral agreements, for instance the 1934 German–Polish Non-Aggression Pact. Though illusions persisted about the League. Toothless international institutions proved useless in the generation before Cato wrote, with the exception of the idealistic Kellogg–Briand Pact of 1928, which renounced war, and laid foundations for some of the indictments at Nuremberg.

The Second World War was to prove the deadliest military conflict in history, with some 60 million dead. This included 383,000 soldiers of Britain and its Empire, and some 67,000 civilian casualties. Would Europe now learn that interdependence, not nationalism, alone could bring peace?

On 19 September 1946, Churchill went to the University of Zurich to speak. 'We must recreate the European family in a regional structure,' he declared, 'it may be, the United States of Europe'. Core to his vision was the ideal that 'there can be no revival of Europe, without a spiritually great Germany'.

Churchill was ambivalent about the extent to which he saw Britain playing an integral part in any United States of Europe. But there was no doubting the tonic his speech gave leaders across Europe. They saw in his vision of greater interdependence the prospect of peace and prosperity. Uniting Western Europe in the face of Stalin's increasingly belligerent Soviet Union, so recently an ally in the Second World War, was a further attraction.

The United States had learnt a lesson: it determined it would not stand apart from Europe as it had done after 1918. Under the 'Marshall Plan', named after Secretary of State George C.

Marshall, it poured $13 billion of aid into the Continent between 1948 and 1952, with West Germany, the principal beneficiary, receiving over a third of this sum. In April 1948, the Organisation for European Economic Cooperation (OEEC, later OECD) was established by the US. Fear of communist parties, particularly in Italy and France, fuelled the US's desire to see pro-capitalist, democratic parties take root. Two months earlier, Britain, France, the Netherlands, Belgium and Luxembourg formed the 'Brussels Treaty Organisation' to pledge mutual military aid and economic support. This paved the way for the establishment of the North Atlantic Treaty Organization (NATO) in April 1949, committing the US to defend peace in Western Europe, the first time in its history it made such a commitment abroad. The following month, the 'Council of Europe' was set up, located in Strasbourg because of its symbolic importance on the Franco-German border. This new body consisted of an initial ten countries, including Britain, and its aim was to uphold human rights, democracy and the rule of law across Europe. It is home to the European Court of Human Rights (ECHR) which enforces the European Convention of Human Rights.

The Labour government of Clement Attlee from July 1945 had a clear preference for 'intergovernmental cooperation', where leaders of the separate nations met together to decide policy, rather than any form of supranationalism or federation, which required pooling of some sovereignty to institutions in Europe. When Churchill returned to No. 10 in October 1951, he appointed some enthusiasts for greater European integration, including the Minister of Housing, Harold Macmillan, and his two sons-in-law, Duncan Sandys and Christopher Soames. Yet despite this, it was soon clear there would be no greater enthusiasm for European federation under Churchill than under the previous Labour government.

The Foreign Office was adamant that 'Great Britain must be viewed as a world power of the second-rank, and not merely a unit in a federated Europe'. One of the leaders of the supranational movement, French Foreign Minister Robert Schuman, proposed a European Coal and Steel Community (ECSC) in May 1950, whose principal aim was to restore economic vitality to West Germany. This would benefit France and the Benelux countries (Netherlands, Belgium and Luxemburg), while ensuring that West Germany looked westwards in building a peaceful post-war order, rather than to the East. Italy was the sixth country to join this new supranational structure, seeing in it the chance to establish political and democratic stability. Jean Monnet, the First President of the ECSC, became one of the principal architects of European federalism and took part in a series of talks to bind the 'ECSC6' closer together.

Britain was wary of these moves towards supranationalism.

Con O'Neill, a diplomat at the British Embassy in West Germany, later recalled of the ECSC: 'I'm ashamed to say that I did not realise its enormous importance ... The idea that there should be a body with real authority over the decisions of national governments was something we felt was grotesque and absurd.' But while the British were remaining spectators on the sidelines, the ECSC6 were stealthily establishing a 'Common Market' in the raw materials advanced industrial nations needed.

Churchill saw his return to power at the age of seventy-six as the chance to re-establish Britain as a great power on the world stage. A year after returning to office, Britain exploded its first atomic bomb and Churchill promptly gave instructions for work to begin on Britain's hydrogen bomb, later detonated in a test in 1957. The breakdown in nuclear cooperation with the United States meant Britain had to work on these projects alone. Churchill struggled largely without success to revive the intimacy and strength of his wartime bond with the US President. It took Britain's membership of the EU for the special relationship to flower again. Britain in the EU mattered to the US.

Britain remained firmly optimistic about finding a post-war role for itself as a proud independent nation. It saw itself as uniquely at the centre of three overlapping circles: the Empire, the US and Europe. So when the decision was taken by the ECSC6 in June 1955 to convene a conference of foreign ministers at Messina in Sicily, led by Paul-Henri Spaak, to discuss further plans for integration and a Common Market, the British did not see this as a major event. The government decided not to send a senior minister or top official, but a junior diplomat called Russell Bretherton. 'He was an obscure middle-ranking official, and that was the point,' wrote Hugo Young.

> His presence at the scene of combat was designed not to accommodate but to insult ... By showing that Europe matters so little to Britain, perhaps Europe would be persuaded that 'Europe' ought not to matter so much to itself. This was the meaning of Bretherton. He was the nominee, void of power or status or the faintest resemblance of the roaring British lion.

Spaak drew up his report on the meeting in November 1955, having been asked to make no reference to Britain's position on the discussions about a Common Market. The six European countries were clear that Britain wanted to absent itself totally from the process. But the ground in Britain was changing. Churchill's successor as Prime Minister from April 1955 to January 1957 was the ill-fated Anthony Eden. The failure of

Eden's disastrous Suez adventure in 1956 damaged Britain's standing in the world and revealed for all to see what a diminished power, militarily and morally, Britain had become. From the deliberations under Spaak, two Treaties of Rome were signed by the six founder members in March 1957. One established the European Economic Community (EEC), the other set up the European Atomic Energy Authority (EAEA).

Britain, beneath its Olympian detachment, was now at a loss about the moves towards integration taking place on the Continent. At the heart of British policy was an enormous hole. Should it join in? Should it observe from the sidelines? Or should it disparage and try to subvert? Britain was not ready emotionally or politically to join in any kind of trade agreement with the defeated. Not even Churchill had seen the way ahead. He epitomised the dilemma for Britain: he did not know what role Britain should have, if any, in the European project, and failed to find the clarity that had so often been his hallmark.

Here was Britain, strong and free, its sovereignty unsullied by Europe, seeking to make its way in the world as a major military, industrial and cultural power, much as the exponents of Brexit believed would happen to Britain once it was finally free of the shackles and chains of the EU. At least Britain had a fall-back plan then. 'Plan G'. What became of it?

CHAPTER VI

BRITAIN'S LATE AND MANGLED JOINING, 1955-1975

SUPPORTING CAST:
Sir Edward Heath

THERE ARE NO HEROES in Britain's protracted joining of the EEC, or common market, nor particular villains. European leaders were thinking of their national, or own self-interest. British leaders were thinking of how they could mitigate Britain's long-term decline. Most put party above national advantage. Few articulated a positive and imaginative vision of Britain working alongside the EEC6, to build mutual prosperity and security and welfare. They were behind the curve, still obsessed by 'winning' the war, receiving the weather blowing across the English Channel, not making it.

Harold Macmillan had his Plan G. Why 'G'? Because the Treasury's options from 'A' to 'F' were considered less

satisfactory as a response to the growing threat from the EEC6.
Plan 'G' was for a European Free Trade Area (EFTA), set up
by the Stockholm Convention in July 1959, with seven signa-
tories: Britain, Austria, Denmark, Norway, Portugal, Sweden
and Switzerland. It established a free trade area to bring down
barriers to trade between member states.

Macmillan's driving obsession was the strategic isolation of
Britain in the post-war world and he saw EFTA, at least in part,
as a way of bolstering Britain's standing. As early as February
1956, before he became Prime Minister, he wrote: 'I do not like
the prospect of a world divided into the Russian sphere, the
American sphere and a United Europe of which we are not a
member.' A year later and now Prime Minister, anxious about
the slow rate of progress of EFTA compared to the EEC, he
wrote: 'What I chiefly fear, and what we must avoid at all costs,
is the [EEC] coming into being and the free trade never following.' He feared it would lead to German domination and 'put us
in a very bad position'.

From 1957 to 1959, Macmillan had put Reginald Maudling in
charge of negotiating a system where the UK could have a free
trade relationship with the EEC (along with the EFTA states),
but not be part of its political structures. It was immensely complicated and did not work. Two of the problems were the very

same ones we are currently experiencing: the half-in countries would have to take rather than make their trade policies, while the EEC6 were unwilling to let others free-ride on their political structures.

Macmillan sensed a real opportunity when the Fourth Republic fell in France in May 1958, and his wartime colleague in north Africa, Charles de Gaulle, became President. He rushed to Paris to visit him, pleading with his old friend to make Anglo-French relations the linchpin of Europe again and asking France to abandon its relationship with the other five in the EEC. As de Gaulle recalled Macmillan saying: 'The Common Market is the Continental System all over again. Britain cannot accept it. I beg you to give it up. Otherwise, we shall be embarking on a war which will doubtless be economic at first but which runs the risk of gradually spreading into other fields.'

But de Gaulle refused to budge. Macmillan's hopes for EFTA were quickly dashed. Within a few months of it being established, it had become clear the dynamism lay in the six countries of the EEC rather than in the seven of EFTA. Macmillan's dismay was recorded in December 1959 when he wrote: 'For the first time since Napoleon, the major continental powers are united in a positive economic grouping, with considerable political aspects, which, though not specifically directed against the United Kingdom, may have the effect of excluding us, both from European markets and from consultation in European policy.' He realised there was no future in his attempt to nudge de Gaulle out of the EEC, nor was the US keen that he even tried to do so. The logic became inescapable. Britain would have to join the EEC.

On 13 July 1960, a key Cabinet meeting was instructed to put in place a process which was to lead to the first application of Britain to join. Two weeks later, a Cabinet reshuffle saw Edward Heath appointed Lord Privy Seal with responsibility for relations with the EEC, while Churchill's two sons-in-law, Christopher Soames and Duncan Sandys, were put respectively in charge of two other departments deemed critical to the success of negotiations: Agriculture and Commonwealth Relations.

John F. Kennedy, as President Eisenhower's successor from January 1961, gave Macmillan a further impetus for joining the EEC. He told him bluntly that Britain was more valuable to his administration as a member than an outsider. But Macmillan faced opposition from within his own party. Many Conservatives had reservations about the impact membership would have on British sovereignty and on Commonwealth trade. The British public too were far from keen. Support for joining peaked in December 1961 at 53 per cent, but by June 1963 this had fallen to a mere 36 per cent. Macmillan became the first of a succession of British Prime Ministers who failed to sell the European ideal to the British public. Most didn't even try.

When de Gaulle rejected Britain's application to join in January 1963, Macmillan confided in his diary: 'French duplicity has defeated us all. All our policies at home and abroad are in ruin.' Heath saw, closer than many, the impact the rejection had on him personally. 'I had terrible difficulties with Macmillan afterwards. He wouldn't do anything, wouldn't concentrate on anything. This was the end of the world.' The rejection of Britain's application, far more than the Profumo sex scandal, accounts for Macmillan's eclipse and his eventual departure from Downing Street in October 1963.

The Conservatives were narrowly defeated by Harold Wilson's Labour party a year later, in October 1964. Richard Crossman, one of Labour's most powerful and articulate spokespersons, retained a 'strongest alone' belief in Britain's place in the world. He told American readers that the Labour Party did not share Conservative pessimism about Britain's place abroad. 'Surely it is a good thing that one of Britain's two great parties is still passionately convinced this country has a future – outside the Common Market,' he wrote. Wilson's ministers were full of optimism that Labour, sweeping away the out-of-touch Tories after 'thirteen wasted years' from 1951 to 1964, would inspire the regeneration and modernisation of British industry, science and society, informed by a commitment to dynamic socialist planning. A general election landslide in March 1966 meant Wilson had a mandate to bring about what many hoped would be Britain's eagerly awaited national renewal.

So what changed? Beneath the surface, Wilson was having doubts about Britain's ability to succeed alone outside the EEC. In October 1966, he called Cabinet to an all-day meeting at Chequers. Preparatory papers included a report from the head of the UK delegation in Brussels, which opened with the words:

for the last twenty years, this country has been adrift. On the whole, it has been a period of decline in our international power and standing. This has helped to produce a national mood of frustration and uncertainty. We do not know where we are going and have begun to lose confidence in ourselves. Perhaps a point has now been reached when the acceptance of a new goal and a new commitment could give the country as a whole a focus around which to crystallise

its hopes and energies. Energy into Europe might provide
the stimulus and the target you require.

Wilson's Cabinet colleagues were mostly unpersuaded by the
argument. But with EFTA transparently proving far less dynamic than the EEC, and with the Commonwealth looking to
markets in the USA and Far East, the EEC option became increasingly persuasive. Earnings in the UK were lagging behind
Europe, rising just 38 per cent in the decade after 1958, compared to 75 per cent in the EEC. Believers in 'Britain alone',
or in the power of socialist planning to provide the catalyst to
science and the economy that Tory free enterprise had not,
began to question their faith.

But for a second time, British application was to be blocked
by de Gaulle's veto in 1967. The French President, addressing
a news conference at the Elysée Palace in Paris on 27 November, accused Britain of a 'deep-seated hostility' and 'lack of
interest' in the EEC. He said that Britain's economy, including its agriculture and working practices, were incompatible
with it. De Gaulle may have had his own ambivalence about
a supranational EEC, but he was convinced that Britain, with
its residual relations with the Commonwealth and the US,
should have no place in it.

Before long, however, events in Western Europe began

moving in favour of Britain joining. De Gaulle resigned as President in April 1969 to be replaced by Georges Pompidou, who was generally supportive of Britain joining. In West Germany, meanwhile, Willy Brandt became the leader of the new Social Democratic government, and felt similarly. Then in June 1970, the increasingly rudderless Wilson was replaced as Prime Minister at the general election by the most Europhile Prime Minister in British history, Edward Heath.

Heath's views about Europe had been forged in the late 1930s. In 1937, he travelled to Germany for the Nuremberg rally, where he met leading Nazis Joseph Goebbels, Hermann Goering and Heinrich Himmler. The next year he was in Barcelona where he was caught up in machine-gun fire during the Spanish Civil War. In the summer of 1939 he travelled to Danzig and Poland with Jewish friend Madron Seligman, returning by rail and hitchhiking across Germany just before the Second World War broke out. It inculcated in him a deep sense that Europe had to work together.

But Britain's Parliament was as divided about Britain joining the EEC at large, and Heath only secured the key vote in parliament in October 1971 by a margin of 356 to 244 MPs, relying upon the support of sixty-nine Labour MPs who defied their party whip to vote for membership. Britain officially entered the EEC on 1 January 1973.

On 3 January, Heath persuaded legendary conductor Her-
bert von Karajan and his Berlin Philharmonic Orchestra to
visit London to celebrate the historic moment. 'My heart was
full of joy that night,' wrote Heath. But as his senior official,
Robert Armstrong, later recalled:

> it always seemed to me that, for him, getting in was an end
> in itself. I did not have the impression that he had at that
> time a coherent vision about what to do with it when we
> were in, how it would evolve and therefore how we would
> try make it develop.

Yet again, we see an absence of clear strategic teaching about
Britain's optimum place in Europe. Heath won the battle. He
did not win the war. His lack of forethought and unsatisfactory
terms on entry, laid up serious problems for the future. A free
market in manufacturing and a protectionist one in agriculture
was hardly optimal for Britain. He was so inept a communi-
cator and strategist that he failed to convince his party or the
country. The great architect of British entry thus is described
as a member of the 'supporting cast' if not a full 'guilty man'.

Had Britain joined under Macmillan or Wilson, it might
have had a far more successful launch. As it was, Britain's
entry on 1 January 1973 coincided with the ending of the

sustained period of economic growth in the EEC countries. The oil price hike later that year was to plunge the world into recession. Worse, Britain entered on terms which France ensured would make it, along with West Germany, the only net budget contributor. It is a matter of conjecture how Britain, with its weak economy, might have weathered the economically turbulent 1970s if outside the EEC.

When Wilson returned to power in March 1974, edging past Heath, he found himself in a dilemma over the fait accompli of Britain's membership of the EEC, despite his having sought membership himself in 1967. Deep opposition to it within his party and the wider Labour movement meant he fell back on promising that a future Labour government would renegotiate the terms of entry and hold a referendum on Britain's continued membership. His attempts to secure a better deal from EEC members was largely unsuccessful, and created enduring doubts among European leaders as to Britain's commitment to the European project. Wilson fared better with his own party and the country at large, refusing to declare his own hand and cajoling his renegotiated terms through a vote in the House of Commons and past a special Labour conference in April 1975. Most of the press and business supported Britain remaining in the EEC, as did most mainstream politicians, including Heath himself, Roy

Jenkins of Labour and Liberal Party leader Jeremy Thorpe. The leaders of the 'no' side were easily portrayed as outliers, including the right-winger Enoch Powell and, from the left of the Labour Party, Tony Benn. The referendum on 5 June was won by a clear margin of 67 per cent to 33 per cent.

CHAPTER VII

THE EMERGENCE OF THE SINGLE CURRENCY, 1979-1992

THE CAST:

M. François Mitterrand, Herr Helmut Kohl

THE SEEDS OF BRITAIN'S departure from the EU, and so many of the tribulations from which the EU suffered in the last two decades, can be traced back to the precipitous, cack-handed way in which the single currency was introduced in the years between 1979 and 1992. Many figures were responsible for the folly, including German Chancellor Helmut Kohl (1982–1998) and French President François Mitterrand (1981–1995), two big men in a big hurry looking for a big legacy.

The British referendum on remaining in the EEC in 1975 resolved absolutely nothing. It led neither to a fresh determination and will in Britain about how to make the most of British membership, now that the electorate had spoken so decisively, nor did it produce among member states a recognition that British political and public opinion had reservations that needed accommodating. As we see repeatedly throughout the EU story, leaders of imagination and insight were lacking.

James Callaghan succeeded Wilson as Prime Minister in April 1976, but he had no desire or ability to embrace a new strategy on the EU. His own reputation among European leaders was poor, stemming from his intransigently pro-British stance in membership negotiations. The British Presidency of the European Council in the first half of 1977, an opportunity for leadership, proved a damp squib, and Britain's relationship with the EEC shambled aimlessly along until Margaret Thatcher succeeded Callaghan as Prime Minister in May 1979, at which point it rapidly deteriorated.

Ideas for an economic and monetary union in Europe can be dated as far back as 1929, when German Chancellor Gustav Stresemann advanced the idea to enhance stability across Europe. The first attempts to explore economic and monetary union within the EEC can be dated to an initiative by a European Commission in December 1969 at The Hague. Reduction of exchange rate volatility was the prime motive. A report from Pierre Werner, Prime Minister of Luxembourg, in October 1970, recommended a centralisation of a macro-economic policy, the fixing of parity rates and liberalisation of capital movement, while falling short of proposing a single currency or central bank. Then President Nixon's removal of gold backing from the US dollar in 1971, and the collapse of the Bretton Woods system, pushed back further discussions for a decade. In March 1979, the European Monetary System (EMS) proposed fixing exchange rates onto the European Currency Unit (ECU) to stabilise exchange rates and to counter inflation. From the early 1980s, discussions over a single currency then came to dominate the political debate in Europe and subsequently in Britain.

The Single European Act of 1986 created the single market. Why, Europeans began to ask with increasing clamour, could there not be a single currency as well? A good question, they thought. There were many arguments against, which were insufficiently heeded. The European Council in Hanover in June 1988 began to explore monetary union and asked European Commission President, Jacques Delors, to chair a committee of central bank governors to examine a timetable and method for creating the European Monetary Union (EMU). Delors had been pushing the idea hard and his report in 1989 duly set out a plan to introduce the EMU. Delors was the driver and, after some convincing, Kohl and Mitterrand stood behind him.

Mitterrand was an enthusiast of the EMU because he saw it

as a way of securing the newly unified Germany within Europe (the Berlin Wall fell in November 1989, with formal reunification following in September 1990). Mitterrand persuaded Kohl that the single currency would be a great legacy they could both have in history, and that he should concede to the end of the Deutschmark in exchange for France's acceptance of German reunification. France's historical and repeated fear of an all-powerful Germany was thus to be mitigated by its entry into a unified currency across much of Europe. The two leaders were in too much of a hurry to permit sufficient harmonisation or the infrastructure ready for a single currency, and the European economies were not ready for it. Fatal mistakes were made by these two big men on the design, including the need for institutional underpinning at the outset. These errors were compounded by others later on, including the Budget rules and the obligation of accession states to join before ready rather than allow a looser federated outer ring.

While Thatcher became increasingly opposed, her two senior ministers, Chancellor Nigel Lawson and Foreign Secretary Geoffrey Howe, became more insistent, pressing her at the June 1989 Madrid summit to set a date for Britain's membership of the Exchange Rate Mechanism (ERM), a prerequisite for Britain adopting the single currency. The ERM had been set up initially by President Valéry Giscard d'Estaing of France and Chancellor Helmut Schmidt; Callaghan decided that Britain would stay outside it, for economic and political reasons. But ten years on, Howe and Lawson thought Britain was ready. Britain joined in October 1990.

Thatcher fell in November of 1989, and John Major succeeded. Over the following two years Britain spent over £6 billion trying to keep sterling within the narrow limits prescribed by the ERM, before being forced to exit on the 16 September 1992 on 'Black Wednesday'. Britain's withdrawal from the ERM was the single most decisive step in Britain's decision to leave the EU twenty-four years later. It fatally weakened Major as Prime Minister: no other subsequent Prime Minister ever dared to stand up and make a consistently positive case for the EU. It emboldened the Eurosceptics who tasted blood and liked it. It educated and unified EU rebels in and outside Parliament to attack and undermine Britain's membership.

Britain's membership was gravely weakened by two big men rushing the EU into an inflexible, ill-considered and premature monetary union.

But British membership was bringing great gains too. Wise leadership could shape and strengthen it.

CHAPTER VIII

THE TWILIGHT YEARS OF THATCHER, 1990-2013

THE CAST:

Baroness Margaret Thatcher

THATCHER IS ONE OF the guiltiest parties of all in the story of Britain and the EU, not for what she did when in office, but for the undermining and galvanising role she assumed after her fall from power in November 1990. After her fractious final months, Britain needed time to establish a settled relationship with the EEC. She could have assisted that process by support from the sidelines. Instead, seething with anger, she launched into the brutal process of undermining her successor on a core government policy, a policy she had spent eleven years crafting.

Thatcher had voted for British entry to the EEC, knowing fully that it had political as well as economic dimensions. In

1975, she said: 'My reasons for staying in [are] ... the ideal and vision of what we could do together if we put as much effort into using our freedom in peacetime as we do to defending it against an obvious foe', and warned of 'the practical consequences that would arise for Britain if, instead of solving our problems as part of a partnership, we withdrew into the unknown'. By temperament, she was always sceptical of the rhetoric surrounding European unity, and was especially concerned by notions of greater federalism. A strong believer in the nation state, her political outlook was defined by national identity. But along with most Conservatives, she shared the instinctive mistrust of ideological nationalism. She thus distanced herself from Enoch Powell, whose diatribe against EEC membership arose from concerns over immigration and sovereignty. She felt enduring bitterness towards Powell for encouraging Tories to vote Labour in February 1974, and never lost her sense that Powell was a treacherous figure who could not be trusted.

Thatcher supported Britain remaining in the EEC in the 1975 referendum, stressing its value in the Cold War context in supporting Western unity. She came later to support enlargement to the south as well as the east, as a force for entrenching democracy and strengthening the West against the Soviet Union. She believed too in the economic case for the EEC, and the positive impact it would have on British industry, as well as being aware of the electoral value of supporting Europe as a weapon against Labour, when it was seen as anti-Europe.

Thatcher arrived at No. 10 in May 1979, generally open-minded and positive about Europe. But her five-year battle to secure justice for Britain in the EEC Budget, that culminated at Fontainebleau in June 1984, engendered enduring resentment. The Budget argument decisively and for ever destroyed her personal pro-EU sentiments. By the end of the five-year slog, any residual goodwill for her fellow European leaders had vanished, and theirs too. After Fontainebleau, she was nevertheless determined to move on and not allow it to define her thinking on Europe. But emotionally, she became stuck.

Thatcher knew what she was signing in the Single European Act in 1986, much the achievement of Delors. She never failed to read the small print, so it is wrong to believe that she nodded through its significant increase in qualified majority voting. Sovereignty for her, unlike for Enoch Powell, was not an absolute, and some diminution of sovereignty was a price worth paying for the economic benefits to Britain that she believed would arise from the creation of the single market.

Her increasing froideur towards the EEC in the latter 1980s began to raise concerns, especially with Geoffrey Howe. For several months, he prodded her to make a 'positive' speech on Europe, suggesting that she use an invitation to talk at Bruges as a platform. Initial indications were that she might do just that, but her hackles were raised when on 6 July 1988 Jacques Delors, President of the EU Commission, told the European Parliament that within ten years he expected 80 per cent of economic legislation, including tax and social policy, to be made within Europe. Then in early September, Delors spoke at a TUC conference in Bournemouth, inviting delegates to join him in becoming 'architects' of Europe, with collective bargaining taking place at European level. Thatcher's speech at Bruges saw her argue that the EEC was strongest when it embraced national traditions without being distracted by utopian ideals: 'We have not successfully rolled back the frontiers in Britain, only to see them re-imposed at a European level with a European superstate, exercising a new dominance from Brussels.'

The speech had much that was encouraging to say about Europe, but it was spun in a way that made it seem almost entirely negative, to the absolute glee of the growing numbers of Eurosceptics, who looked to her as the legitimiser and champion of their nationalistic crusade. The speech sowed the seeds of her own downfall, as Howe later wrote: 'I can now see that [the Bruges speech] was probably the moment in which there began to crystallise the conflict of loyalty with which I was to struggle for perhaps too long.' Two years later, Howe delivered his speech in Parliament which triggered a leadership election and Thatcher's ousting. Yet the Bruges speech was never a manifesto for British withdrawal, or for calling into question Britain's continuing membership. It was the moment when Thatcher chose to confront, very publicly, creeping European federalism. She subsequently had the opportunity to contextualise her comments, and distance herself from the firebrands who seized on her words. She chose to let the opportunity pass by.

Her final months were dominated by struggle. By now, she was fighting most members of her Cabinet, and only with deep reluctance did she agree to Britain's accession to the ERM in October 1990. She developed a visceral hatred to the whole concept, and later said that the European single currency was an attempt to create a 'European superstate' and would fail 'economically, politically and socially'.

German reunification troubled her deeply too in her final months in power. She was implacably opposed to reunification, above all on the timescale that Helmut Kohl envisaged. She harboured a great fear of a reunified Germany, and was apprehensive about German dominance within the EEC, particularly economic dominance. A famous seminar was convened at Chequers in March 1990 for heavyweight thinkers to try to persuade her to adopt a more positive attitude towards German reunification. But the leaking of some unflattering remarks about the German national character exposed her antagonism.

Thatcher's story up until 1990 was one of increasing disillusion with the EEC. Many of her concerns were legitimate, including her distrust of the single currency. The one error she made as Prime Minister was insufficiently to stress the positives of British membership, economically, politically and culturally: and when she did, as in the Bruges speech, to make the remarks appear anything more than lip service.

The problems came after her fall from power in November 1990. The great leader now had no future. Being Prime Minister had been her whole existence. Her obsession left her bereft during the last twenty-three years of her life after she left office. She blamed Europe to a large extent for her downfall, seeing it as the dividing line between her and the Cabinet. In retirement a fundamentalist anti-EU position rapidly became her *raison d'être*, a stance that all her supporters could understand. Overnight she had her cause, a simple, clear rallying point that was to provide comfort in the long and empty years to come.

Her closest advisers after 1990 were anti-EU to a remarkable degree. None more than Robin Harris, an active companion on her journey towards a breach with the EU, a breach that grew wider until Britain, almost inevitably, voted to leave. Harris, unlike Thatcher, was an ideological rather than a pragmatic nationalist. Thatcher's new thinking took shape in a speech at The Hague in May 1992, with its theme of the EEC as 'yesterday's future'. Charles Powell, her former No. 10 private secretary, tried to moderate her views and to limit the damage she was causing her successor, John Major. But while he was successful in stopping her making derogatory comments about Major's attempts to bring peace to Northern Ireland, he had no success on Europe. She was unstoppable.

In no time at all, she lost faith in Major, whom she had anointed as her successor. She forgot everything she had said and believed about the contempt she felt for her predecessor Edward Heath, for the way he denigrated her and her leadership. Thatcher now repeated the same behaviour with her own successor, with far more menacing and deadly impact. She held court in temporary residence at Westminster's Great College Street, to which critics of the EEC and of Major

flocked, lapping up her every word. Her disparaging comments soon found their way into the press.

She was anxious not to destabilise him for the general
election in April 1992, aware of the damage it would do to
the party and her own standing among Conservatives. But
two weeks after polling day, she pounced, venting her frustration in an interview to the US magazine *Newsweek*, an
interview she gave in her home, not at the office, fully aware
of the damage that it would do to her successor. The first
volume of her memoirs, *The Downing Street Years*, published
in 1993 caused upset, but not nearly as much as the second
volume, published in 1995. By then, she was utterly disillu-
sioned. She was openly scathing about Major's domestic and
European policy.

The Maastricht Treaty debates became the public platform
for Thatcher to vent her concerns about the government's
European Policy. Her dignity as a leader, and her objectivity,
were diminished by her personal bitterness and desire for
revenge. She legitimised Euroscepticism in the Tory Party.
Though she had little taste for Maastricht rebels personally, regarding most of them as beneath her, by lending her
intellectual and personal authority to a raft of individuals
across the whole spectrum of right-wing persuasions, she
achieved far more influence and did far more damage to the

country she loved than the man whose actions she abhorred, Enoch Powell.

It is extremely unlikely that Thatcher added one iota to her stature by what she chose to do after leaving office. Thatcher led one of the most radical governments in British history but was there another Prime Minister before her who so diminished their reputation after leaving office?

CHAPTER IX

JOHN MAJOR'S BASTARDS, 1990–1997

THE CAST:

Baroness Margaret Thatcher, Lord Norman Tebbit

SUPPORTING CAST:

Mr James Goldsmith

JOHN MAJOR IS THE only Prime Minister in this book who emerges with credit, at a very considerable personal cost. He tried to give priority to the national interest and to find a 'middle course' for Britain in the EU. The opt-outs he secured in the Maastricht Treaty might have formed the basis for a long-term British policy to the European Union (EU), as it became officially known when Maastricht came into force in 1993.

Major's task was made more difficult because the
sands under him were shifting. Labour, sceptical towards
Europe under the leaderships of Harold Wilson (1963–76),
James Callaghan (1976–79) and Michael Foot (1980–83),
shifted its approach under Neil Kinnock (1983–92) and Tony
Blair (1994–2007). Labour's switch to a positive espousal of
Europe paved the way for a clear line of attack for the Tories
by embracing an increasingly popular Eurosceptic cause.
The European project moreover was changing, principally
due to economic and monetary union, and the increasing
federalism gave critics much more red meat to sink their
teeth into. The balance of opinion in the Conservative Party
was thus tilted towards Euroscepticism under Major, among
ministers, backbenchers, as well as in the country.

Eurosceptic animals were of four breeds, though many
were mongrels, fitting the characteristics of more than one
breed. Some had been opposed from the outset, such as John
Biffen and Teddy Taylor. Others stressed the threat to national
sovereignty, including Bill Cash and Richard Shepherd. Free
marketeers saw the EU as damaging Britain's capitalist potential – 'socialism by the back door', as Thatcher put it. This was
the largest group, including John Redwood and Iain Duncan
Smith. Finally, were the populist nationalists such as Teresa
Gorman and Tony Marlow. The most vociferous and angry

of them all was Norman Tebbit – a big beast – who set himself up as the populist leader determined to destroy Major and his European policy under any circumstances. His nationalism was ideological in the Enoch Powell sense; his style was rabble-rousing in the Nigel Farage sense. With his patron and idol Thatcher deposed, he was angry: he was now an outsider. A dangerous place for him to be.

These MPs would have served their party and their country better if, rather than promulgating a distorted and negative image of the EU's impact on Britain, they had given their time to causes that the public were concerned about, including education, health, the environment, infrastructure and inequality. Instead, they built their careers on a half-truth at best.

Major was chosen as leader in part because he was a compromise candidate, less Europhile than Douglas Hurd and Michael Heseltine. As Major said of himself in 1981, he was neither Europhile nor Europhobe, or as he put it: 'I'm not going to get into the Eurosceptic–Euro-enthusiast argument. I am a Euro-realist. I think that is the position of most people in the country.' He believed that Britain's position in Europe could best be advanced not by standing aside, but by arguing for Britain's interests and values at the heart of the EU's decision-making bodies. Several gains that Britain obtained from the

EU had come from arguing at the centre, including the lower-
ing of tariffs and opening up of European markets to the rest of
the world, as well as making the EU more pro-American, more
pro-free trade and more pro-free competition. Enlargement,
equally, would not have happened to the degree it did without
Britain's input. As Major said, there were just three strategic
options available for Britain towards the EU: 'To leave, which
is unthinkable; to stand aside and let ourselves be dragged
along by others, which is untenable, or to be at the very heart
of the Community and help frame the decisions – which is
our policy.'

If Major was to achieve his middle way, he needed constructive support from Whitehall and from finance and business,
as well as from the main political parties in Westminster. But
Labour played politics, while his own party systematical-
ly undermined him, spurred on by his General, Thatcher,
Lieutenant, Tebbit, and an army of excitable Eurosceptic
squaddies. Major found himself constantly having to make
compromises. Ken Clarke's criticism of this tactic – 'If you give
half an inch to those characters, they'll end up taking a foot' –
was fair but did not take account of Major's limited freedom
of manoeuvre.

Major enjoyed relative tranquillity only in his first few
weeks in power after November 1990. On 23 March 1991, he

travelled to Bonn and announced his vision for Britain 'where we belong, [at] the very heart of Europe'. He received a savage response from Eurosceptics, which he described as 'twisted and distorted'. Tebbit emerged then as his key critic, writing in *The Guardian* that the 'present government has no mandate to give away the right of the British people to self-government'.

The conference at Maastricht in December 1991 saw Major achieve several compromises which he hoped would be sufficient to secure the overwhelming support of the middle ground in British politics. They included an opt-out from the Social Chapter, which Thatcher had characterised as socialist, the right for Parliament to decide whether Britain would enter the single currency, the retention of some control of security forces across Europe, the advancement of the notion of 'subsidiarity' and intergovernmental rather than supranational cooperation as the basis of deciding domestic defence and foreign policy. Even Boris Johnson described it as 'a copybook triumph for Mr Major'. Only seven of forty expected dissenters failed to support it in parliament in December 1991. Criticism was muted before the general election in April 1992. The view emerged soon after on the right that Major's pragmatism was a weakness, and that neither he nor his compromises could be trusted. When the Maastricht Treaty was signed nevertheless in February, the expectation was that it would come into force on 1 January in 1993, and that ratification by parliament would be a formality.

Denmark's rejection of the Maastricht Treaty in a referendum in June 1992 proved the catalyst for dissent to breach out into the open. Norman Lamont, Major's Chancellor (1990–93), said the Danish rejection was 'better' than the Conservatives' general election victory earlier in the year. Black Wednesday ('White Wednesday' to Eurosceptics) in September was described by Charles Moore, then editor of the *Daily Telegraph*, as a defeat 'almost as complete as is possible, in peace time, to conceive'. Tebbit told journalists that the responsibility for Britain's rejection rested primarily with Major for dragging the Conservatives into the ERM when he had been Chancellor. At the party conference that October in Brighton, it was feared Tebbit would go to the press if denied the chance to speak. Having secured his way to the platform, he told the delegates: 'This conference wants policies for Britain first, Britain second, and Britain third.' He whipped the Eurosceptic factions into a fervour, inviting audience participation, evincing shouts of 'NO' to a succession of questions: 'Do you want to be citizens of Europe, to see a single currency, to let other countries decide Britain's immigration controls?' Nationalism was what Tebbit wanted. The more discerning lowered their heads, embarrassed: Cato could have told them about effective audience manipulation in a different age.

The eventual passage of the Maastricht Treaty after months of torrid and increasingly bitter fighting came after a 'no confidence' vote on 23 July 1993. The day after, Major was unwittingly recorded responding to questions asking why he did not just sack rebel Cabinet ministers, including Peter Lilley, Michael Portillo and John Redwood: 'I could bring in other people, but where do you think most of this poison is coming from? From the dispossessed and the never-possessed ... We don't want another three bastards out there.' His comments inflamed passions still further. The right became even more convinced he had to go.

Bill Cash set up the 'European Foundation', a think tank to push Eurosceptic policies. The Anti-Federalist League, which ultimately led to the creation of the UK Independence Party, was another body founded at this time. Then in 1994, businessman James Goldsmith personally pledged £20 million for the formation of the 'Referendum Party' to press for a referendum on Britain's continued membership in the EU. An ardent protectionist and anti-German, he was concerned about his personal business interests and German hegemony. The Referendum Party, another forerunner of UKIP, received over 800,000 votes in the 1997 general election, 2.6 per cent of the overall vote – buying influence to damage Britain's membership of the EU has a long history.

Major experienced many further humiliations in his final years in power. The passage of the European Finance Bill at the end of 1994, which saw the withdrawal of the Conservative whip from eight Tory MPs, was one of the bitterest. Tebbit indicated the whipless MPs had his and Lady Thatcher's full backing. In an interview with David Frost to mark the publication of the second volume of her memoirs, Thatcher described the withdrawal of the whip as 'absurd', denounced Major for repeatedly saying 'yes' to Europe, and criticised the government for being insufficiently Conservative.

When Cash introduced a Bill calling for a referendum on Europe, Thatcher invited him for lunch in her office in Belgravia and promised to make a substantial donation to his European Foundation, to replace the money that he had been told he could not receive from Goldsmith. Thatcher, once disgusted by Powell's recommendation to vote Labour, began to speak admiringly of Blair, whose team cleverly courted her. Major felt inwardly betrayed. His public response was understated: 'Everyone must answer for her own actions. Personally, I would have given the money to the Conservative Party.' At the 1997 general election, Thatcher implied she would not campaign herself for Conservatives in seats where there was a candidate from Goldsmith's Referendum Party.

Blair won by a landslide. Britain's policy towards the EU never recovered credibility or coherence after the seven years of bloody infighting.

CHAPTER X

BALONEY AND BANANAS,
1990–2015

THE CAST:

Mr Rupert Murdoch, Mr Paul Dacre, Mr Boris Johnson

SUPPORTING CAST:

Lord Black of Crossharbour, Mr Richard Desmond,
the Barclay brothers

THE PRESS HAS POWER without responsibility, to borrow a phrase from Rudyard Kipling, borrowed by Stanley Baldwin in 1931. Influential figures within it wilfully distorted the truth for reasons of personal or corporate advantage, and in some instances ideology, giving a one-sided view of the value of the European Union to Britain. We can never know for sure what impact they had on the formation of public opinion. But press headlines determine the agenda of the BBC and other broadcasters. They are read in No. 10. They count.

The British press had not always been anti-EU. At the time of the 1975 referendum, when the EU was still known as the EEC, all mainstream titles were pro-remaining, including the *Daily Mail*, the *Daily Telegraph*, the *Daily Express* and *The Sun*, as well as *The Times*, *The Guardian*, the *Financial Times* and the *Daily Mirror*. The dissenting outlets were from the far left, above all the *Morning Star*. The daily circulation of the pro-EU outlets was some 15 million, while those against the EU sold fewer than 150,000.

The change in tone can be dated to 1979, the year that Margaret Thatcher came to power, and the year that Rupert Murdoch took over as chairman and chief executive of News Corporation. In 1981, Murdoch bought *The Times*. As Thatcher became increasingly Eurosceptic, Tory newspapers took their lead from her: if she had sung a different song, they would have sung it too. *The Times* and *Sunday Times*, as well as *The Sun* and *News of the World* under Murdoch became staunch supporters of Thatcher and more strongly anti-European. The *Daily Telegraph* remained more even-handed, but a key moment came after Boris Johnson, sacked from *The Times* in 1988 for falsifying information, was appointed Europe correspondent for the *Daily Telegraph*. Martin Fletcher, subsequent

Brussels correspondent for *The Times*, wrote an article for the *New York Times*, recalling how Johnson

made his name in Brussels not with honest reporting but with remorseless Euroscepticism, tirelessly attacking, mocking and denigrating the EU. He wrote about the EU's plans to ban Britain's favourite potato chips, standardise condom sizes and blow up its own asbestos-filled head-quarters. These articles were undeniably colourful but bore scant relation to the truth.

Who cared? It sold copies. The public devoured it. Before long, editors at other newspapers started pressing their own correspondents to match Johnson's colourful reports in con-trast to the usual dry-as-dust Brussels reporting.

Johnson's stories were given headlines including: 'Brussels recruits sniffers to ensure that Euro-manure smells the same', 'Threat to British pink sausages' and 'Snails are fish, says EU'. Johnson saw it himself as a jolly jape, a kind of game, telling the BBC years later:

[I] was sort of chucking these rocks over the garden wall and I listened to this amazing crash from the greenhouse next door, over in England as everything I wrote from

Brussels was having this amazing, explosive effect on the
Tory Party – and it really gave me this, I suppose, rather
weird sense of power.

His editor Max Hastings was not a fan of this kind of journalism
but to proprietor Conrad Black, Johnson and his weird sense of
power became an untouchable: he was his favourite journalist.
Euroscepticism saved Johnson's career and set it on an upward
trajectory. When Charles Moore succeeded Hastings as editor
in 1995, the *Daily Telegraph* became still more Eurosceptic.
Johnson became 'a hate figure in Brussels', according to journalist and author Alan Philps, and the darling of the right. But
his journalism was irresponsible, deceitful and frivolous.

Charles Moore later admitted: 'We were probably rather boring
on the subject [of Europe] and made ourselves a notice board. I
do regret the factional negativity that crept in over Europe. It isn't
good for papers to bash all the time.' But the damage had been
done, whatever Moore's regrets. His predecessor, Max Hastings,
much more of a pragmatic figure who supported Europhile
Douglas Hurd for the Conservative Party leadership in 1990, left
in part because of what some believe to have been intrusive inter-
ference from the proprietor, Conrad Black.

Black is an intriguing figure, who in 2007 was forced
out by shareholders, convicted of fraud and sentenced to

four-and-a-half years in prison. After his release, he was still railing against the EU, writing of 'the anti-democratic nature of the Brussels authority that intrudes more and more constantly into the lives of average people ... This imposition has grated steadily on the British, from the display of bananas in super-markets to the (one-size-fits-all) size of condoms.' In 2004, the reclusive Barclay brothers, who have some £6 billion of wealth, bought the Telegraph Group, which included *The Spectator*. They appear to have sought it as a trophy, as was also the case with their purchase of the Ritz Hotel. The word that came down to staff as the reclusive brothers' approach was that the titles should celebrate enterprise and commerce. There was very little change to direction, or clarity about why they had bought the newspaper group. The *Telegraph* has continued to be successful, though the objectivity and quality of its journal-ism has been compared unfavourably to the paper's golden era, when it was edited by Hastings and Moore, and before them, by legendary journalist Bill Deedes (1974–86). Pro-EU busi-ness and financial content has found it difficult to find space on the *Telegraph's* comment pages or indeed in its news sections.

The Sun turned nastier as the 1990s wore on, following Thatcher's lead in treating the EU as an enemy, with no hint of restraint. Beneath the notorious 'Up Yours Delors' headline of November 1990 it asked:

Its patriotic family of readers to tell the feelthy French to FROG OFF! They INSULT us, BURN our lambs, FLOOD our country with dodgy food and PLOT to abolish the dear old pound. Now it's your turn to kick THEM in the Gauls ... Remember folks, it won't be long before the garlic-breathed bastilles will be here in droves once the Channel Tunnel is open. So, grab your megaphones ... and let 'em hear the British lion ROAR.

In its issue of 21 November 1994, *The Sun*'s headline was 'Now They've Really Gone Bananas: Euro bosses ban "too bendy" ones and set up minimum shop size of five-and-a-half inches'. Distortions and half-truths eventually came to dominate the headlines in other titles too: 'EU Judges want Sharia Law applied in British Courts' said the *Daily Mail* in April 2009, 'EU's plan to liquefy corpses and pour them down the drain', said the *Daily Express* on 8 July 2010, while the *Daily Telegraph* said in October 2011, 'Children to be banned from blowing up balloons, under EU safety rules'. All of these were distortions.

Visceral hatred of the EU across the press is unique to Britain. The odd title in Scandinavia, the Netherlands, Germany and elsewhere can be hostile, but there is nothing like the consistency and strength of the hostility seen in Britain. Why might this be the case? Many proprietors, editors and individual journalists have their own strongly held beliefs against the EU, and a desire to see British sovereignty remain intact. But beyond this lies a struggle for influence. The more the press feared power shifting to Europe, the more they saw their own power dwindling.

Press owners and editors crave influence, and want to see No. 10 dancing to their tune. Brussels is remote and dull to them, and Britain has only one voice among twenty-eight. The British press is focused on Westminster and Whitehall, and many in it resent Brussels. Stories knocking Europe sell, as academic and a founder of Hacked Off, the group campaigning for media accountability, Brian Cathcart notes: 'When it comes to selling newspapers, xenophobia, racism, jingoism are very helpful. In a complicated world, there is nothing simpler than to identify a faceless foreign baddie, and blame everything on them.'

Why would editors and proprietors want to support any policy that threatened to leech power away from Westminster, Whitehall and No. 10? It explains why virtually no Prime Minister, Foreign Secretary nor government since Thatcher's has been happy to give a positive vision of Europe, and why almost all have been happy to connive in seeing it as a scapegoat. The EU, faceless and amorphous, has been unable to defend itself.

No two figures have been more significant in shaping British thinking on the EU than Paul Dacre and Rupert Murdoch. In 1992, Dacre became editor of the *Daily Mail* and in 1998, editor-in-chief of the Mail Group. The EU stands for everything he dislikes most. He sees Britain as under threat by a liberal elite in Brussels that wants to impose foreign values. Where Murdoch's priority is always to improve the climate for his business, Dacre is far more visceral and emotional. Under him, the *Mail* has encouraged readers to think that the problems Britain faces are all the fault of an alien institution, the EU, and once relieved of it, Britain will be truly great again. The *Daily Mail* is the second biggest-selling newspaper in the country after *The Sun*, and thanks largely to the journalistic flair and drive of Dacre, its influence far outstrips its readership. It is often the first paper turned to in successive No. 10s, as well as by editors of BBC Radio 4's *Today* programme. Commentators are torn between their admiration for Dacre's undoubted skill at selling newspapers and touching the popular nerve, and their abhorrence of his newspapers' remorseless negativity and hostility.

None of the above titles have been more virulent in opposition to the EU than the *Daily Express*, described as 'the UKIP of the press'. According to Cathcart, despite the *Daily Express* having a small circulation, 'the *Mail* and *The Sun* look over their shoulders at it because they fear being out-righted. They think, "we don't want them to have a stronger line than ours.

We can't look wimpish when compared to them.'" Richard Desmond acquired the Express newspaper titles, including the *Daily Star*, in 2000. Desmond's early career was in pornography, including titles such as *Readers Wives* and *Electric Blue*. He told *Guardian* journalist Decca Aitkenhead that he hated being referred to as a pornographer: 'To me, pornography's illegal, druggy, back streets, prostitution, you know … To me we were the publishers of adult magazines. That's it.' When asked if he watches it, he responded: 'Definitely. Everyone should watch it.'

In 2014, Desmond gave UKIP £300,000, and donated £1 million the following year. 'I firmly believe in UKIP. It's a party for good, ordinary British people. It is not run by elitists.' He is reported to hector staff and regularly use expletives. According to *The Observer* in 2001, a female executive, six months pregnant, was told by Desmond: 'Tell these people how much I am f***ing paying you.' The report went on to claim: 'Executives are abused in punishingly long editorial meetings, Desmond only stopping while a butler shimmers in bearing a banana on a plate. The press baron consumes the banana and then continues on the attack.'

Perhaps it was a bent EU banana. Desmond might retort that the story above was baloney as well.

Studies can never prove conclusively the impact of thirty

years of hostile reporting, exaggeration and untruths. But by the time the referendum campaign opened in 2016, decades of negativity about Britain's place within Europe could not be undone.

And who are these men (no women) who have had so much power over ordinary British people? An Australian tycoon, a master of frivolity, a Canadian fraudster, an angry nostalgic, two recluses and a pornographer-denier.

These are the men who poisoned Britain's understanding of the EU.

CHAPTER XI

BLAIR DUCKS THE ADVOCACY, 1997-2007

THE CAST:

Mr Anthony Blair, Mr Rupert Murdoch

'IF YOU SEIZE THIS moment, then you can shape events and not have events shape you', veteran pro-European Roy Jenkins told Blair in October 1997. 'I will be very blunt on this. You have to choose between leading in Europe or having Murdoch on your side. You can have one but not both.'

Jenkins was right. Blair had to choose. He had already secured Murdoch's backing before the 1997 election. Could he now become the long needed, popular advocate for an EU that Murdoch so despised?

Three months before the Jenkins conversation, Blair had just returned from an intergovernmental conference in Amsterdam. Buoyed by his success in retaining powers for

Britain over taxation and borders, while charming the pants off his fellow European leaders, he was in an expansive mood. He rolled up his sleeves and went for a walk in the garden at No. 10 with his now Cabinet Secretary Richard Wilson. 'The Germans lost the war and have got over it. The French were humiliated and have got over it', the Prime Minister told him. 'The British won the war and never got over it. My generation do not have the same hang-ups about Europe as older generations. My job is to establish a lasting relationship, and lead Britain in Europe.'

Blair went on to achieve much in Europe. Britain was a leading player in several core EU decisions during his ten years, including the Saint-Malo declaration signed in December 1998 with French President Jacques Chirac, which created a European security and defence policy including a European military force. Blair played a key role in helping launch the Lisbon process to facilitate the internal market and competitiveness on treaty reform policy and enlargement, and making intergovernmental discussions between national leaders more productive. Blair substantially improved the dialogue and relationships between Britain and its EU partners, and made them increasingly sympathetic to the 'Anglo-social' model, where a dynamic market economy is coupled with protection for vulnerable workers, tax credits and the minimum wage. No other Prime Minister has been so adept at establishing good personal relationships across Europe.

Blair saw his failure to introduce the euro as a great mistake. He was blocked twice by his Chancellor, Gordon Brown, on Britain adopting the euro, in 1997 and 2003. But to have introduced the euro, a fundamentally misconceived project, would have been a grave handicap for Britain. His 'failure' was Britain's escape.

Blair's second error, enlargement, was a success in many ways, but it had a significant downside. By opting not to take advantage of the seven-year transitional period before free movement began in earnest, in contrast to France and Germany which did, he opened Britain up to a mass influx of EU immigration. The government, not opposed by the Conservatives, decided that so long as migrants wanted to come to Britain and contribute to the economy, they would be welcome, filling vitally needed vacancies and paying taxes. Additionally, those who had lived behind the Iron Curtain now had the right to share in the British dream.

Unexpectedly large numbers flocked to Britain and Ireland, which had relatively deregulated economies and an abundance of low-paid, unskilled jobs. Blair later admitted the volume took him by surprise. The English language proved an additional allure to young migrants, eager to get on in the world. But the numbers coming in disturbed the equilibrium in certain communities across the country, and paved the way for the reaction that reared its head in a surge of nationalism especially after the 2008 financial crisis. His opening of British borders 'transformed many British communities, changed the labour market and broke any bond of trust voters had with their leaders', as an editorial titled 'Blair caused Brexit' put it in the *Daily Telegraph*.

But the biggest failure of Blair's European policy was neither enlargement nor the euro. It was his unwillingness to persuade the public of the benefits of Britain's membership of the EU. Very few Prime Ministers have possessed Blair's charismatic powers of persuasion. If anyone was capable of convincing an electorate that the downsides, including losses of sovereignty, were more than balanced by the benefits that EU membership brought, it was Blair.

But he ducked the opportunity to become a powerful advocate for the EU. Why?

'I've no doubt at all that Britain's future lies in Europe', Blair wrote in 1993. After he became Labour leader in 1994, he spoke of the importance of Britain being a key member of the EU: 'It's one of those issues where you have to mark your line, then stick to it through thick and thin.'

In July 1995, Blair was invited by Murdoch to speak at a conference for senior executives of News Corporation at Hayman Island, a resort off the coast of Queensland, Australia. 'I think Rupert and the company took it as a sign of courtesy and also [found it] rather flattering that he'd flown halfway around the world to be there,' said Murdoch's right-hand man, Irwin Stelzer. Like Blair, Cameron missed opportunities to challenge and contest the Euroscepticism of the press barons, pandering to them instead, offering an unrealistic promise to renegotiate free movement.

In the 1997 general election, *The Sun* endorsed Labour, which Blair's press supremo, Alastair Campbell, once described as his biggest achievement in politics. Murdoch's support came at a price. On St George's Day, 23 April 1997, Blair wrote in *The Sun*: 'I didn't make my position on Europe absolutely clear. I will have no truck with a European super-state. If there are moves to create that dragon, I will slay it.' Perhaps his change of tack on Europe was understandable ahead of the general election.

But Blair's Labour Party won 418 and 413 seats respectively in the general elections of 1997 and 2001, the only occasions since the Second World War when a party has achieved over 400 seats. He could have chosen to ignore Murdoch and his

Euroscepticism. He did not. He rarely gave pro-European speeches. His most important speeches on Europe as Prime Minister, such as in June 1998 when he urged the EU to reform itself to become more democratic and accountable, and said that he would lead Britain into a more constructive relationship with Europe, typically were made abroad, as on this occasion in Strasbourg.

Blair could have been the hero of Britain's place in the EU, defining the relationship as no other Prime Minister has ever managed to do so. Had he expended a fraction of the energy he used persuading the country about Iraq on selling them the value to Britain of the EU, then British history could have been very different. As it was, the erosion of trust in him over Iraq meant that when the voice of a former Labour leader was most needed during the referendum campaign, no one was listening to him. Iraq blighted Blair's prospects of becoming EU President in 2009, but if he had become President, he might just have been able to coax the EU back towards the Anglo-Saxon model.

With ten years at the helm with massive majorities and a strong and secure economy, Blair had an unrivalled opportunity to reshape public thinking and encourage a reasoned understanding of the value of the EU to Britain to take root.

No other Prime Minister since 1973 was blessed with the same opportunities. No other British Prime Minister was regarded with as much respect in Europe.

Part of the blame for the failure of Blair's advocacy lay in the EU itself and its failures to reform, to listen and to be flexible.

CHAPTER XII

BLINKERED BRUSSELS, 1985–2015

SUPPORTING CAST:

M. Jacques Santer, epitomising EU apparatchiks at their most ineffectual; S. Silvio Berlusconi, epitomising EU national leaders at their most negligent

THE EU IN ITS early manifestations was brought together by big figures, Jean Monnet, Paul-Henri Spaak and Robert Schuman, as well as by giants who were national leaders, Konrad Adenauer of Germany and Charles de Gaulle of France. From the 1980s onwards, Europe was overseen by a series of mainly little men (there were no women). There were some big ideas, but few big people. When the EU most needed figures of intellectual brilliance and depth of imagination, it produced just pygmies. These men were guilty not just of lack of imagination, but often of arrogance and the

failure of leadership. Too many took decisions predominantly in the interests of their own career, ignoring the wishes of
increasingly disengaged, baffled and sceptical member nations and their populations. They were guilty of arrogance
and hubris.

In January 1985, Jacques Delors of France became the
eighth President of the EEC commission. The Single European Act of 1986 was the biggest step towards a deeper union
since the signing of the Treaty of Rome in 1957. In Thatcher's Bruges speech of September 1998, she gave a prescient
warning that the EEC was becoming a 'narrow-minded, inward-looking club'. The clear danger was that Europe was
equating strengthening its institutions with a common European identity which lacked the basis in national legitimacy and
national democratic will. Thatcher's speech was viewed in
Brussels less as fair comment than as petulance and anger by
a rogue woman. Brussels was introspective and self-regarding
when it needed to reach out across the expanding nations of
the EU. Promotion was on the basis of extolling the virtues of
greater European unification rather than speaking of the need
for securing the willing agreement of national leaders and
populations across the EU.

This wider consciousness was needed because, as we
have seen, by the late 1980s, the pace of reform was moving

at an unstoppable speed. German reunification, which saw its population rise to 80 million, 20 million more than in Britain, France and Italy, made it unambiguously the first among equals in the twelve EU nations. Brussels and key European leaders, above all in France, saw the solution to Germany unbalancing the EU in accelerating the pace of greater integration. Kohl, one of the main architects of this strategy, repeatedly used the metaphor 'the German house must be built under a European roof'. In June 1985, the Benelux countries, Germany and France, signed the Schengen Agreement, confirming that they would abolish all internal borders before January 1993. At the Dublin summit in June 1990, the EC12 committed to moving the community 'from an enlightened entity primarily based on economic integration and political cooperation into a political union'. A clause too far.

The Maastricht Treaty process of 1991–93 for monetary union was the most egregious example of an arrogant disregard for the views of citizens across the EU. It brought division and widespread suffering in southern nations in particular in its wake. Little effort was made to discover what the citizens of the new European Union wanted, or to make the pace of the introduction of the single currency, a flawed project intrinsically, more flexible and manageable. Balefully inadequate thought was put into explaining what the initiatives were, and why they were needed. High politics, not democratic account-ability, dictated Maastricht. So much for subsidiarity, one of the aims of Maastricht, which sought to render EU decisions less remote from the citizens. Maastricht created the European Central Bank (ECB) and European System of Central Banks (ECSB). By insulating them from democratic accountability, and denying the power of national legislatures to amend their powers, the 'democratic deficit' in the EU was significantly extended.

The 1990s offered swathes of instances where the EU was complacent, overly complex and distant from voters. The Danish 'no' vote to Maastricht had been a harbinger of nation-al concerns whose significance was ignored. In 1995, Jacques Santer of Luxembourg replaced Delors as President of the Commission. He surrounded himself with high-profile pol-iticians and big egos and in this era the Commission became notorious for abuse of public funds through cronyism and nep-otism. An independent inquiry in 1999 found serious lapses in professionalism: former French Prime Minister Edith Cresson (1991–92) appointing a provincial dentist and personal friend as a highly paid adviser was yet another gift to EU haters in the press. The inquiry's report concluded that 'it is difficult to find anyone who has even the slightest sense of responsibility' for the abuses uncovered. The commission resigned en masse.

Britain could have filled the vacuum. But, as the *Sunday Times* put it, 'we chose not to lead in the EU but to accept a loss of influence, including in a Brussels bureaucracy once heavily influenced by senior British officials'.

The Amsterdam Treaty of 1997 saw Schengen absorbed into the EU framework and a new 'High Representative' created to oversee EU foreign and defence policy. But Amsterdam failed to deal with many of the institutional and democratic questions posed by enlargement. Direct elections every five years to the European Parliament had been introduced in 1979, again with the groundwork among member nations wholly inadequate, with the result that voting for Members of European Parliament (MEPs) never caught the popular imagination. Lessons were not learnt about how to make the elections more meaningful and attractive to voters across Europe. Even twenty years later, in June 1999, widespread apathy and dissatisfaction among European voters was evident, with Britain recording the lowest turnout in a national election, at just 24 per cent, since the birth of democracy. Even in Germany, less than half of the electorate (45 per cent) chose to vote: a fall of 15 per cent compared to the elections of 1989 and 1994.

Enlargement, a massive change to the entire structure of the EU, whatever the merits, lacked democratic support from across EU nations. Britain pushed strongly for countries in the newly free Central and Eastern Europe to join, while the French were far more reluctant. Suddenly, with a big bang, ten new countries joined the EU in 2004, with more joining in 2007 and 2013, notably Bulgaria, Romania, and Croatia, which barely met the criteria for entry and who still have difficulty coping with membership today.

The Constitutional Convention from 2001 then ditched the pillared structure of Maastricht in favour of advocating a more centralised EU with a strengthened commission and a permanent presidency. In July 2003, the European Council Presidency passed to one of the most unsavoury leaders that European politics has seen in the past twenty-five years, Silvio Berlusconi. Hopes that the EU would have the imagination and integrity to adapt itself to gain popular support and legitimacy across Europe faded at the hands of the maestro of the 'Bunga-Bunga party'. The Lisbon Treaty of December 2007, which concluded the constitutional process, was another opportunity lost for reforming EU institutions and ministries. Lisbon gave more power to the European Parliament and majority voting, taking significant steps in the direction of enhanced EU federalism. Where were the big men and women when the EU needed them? In their place was Santer and Berlusconi.

Agriculture has been another area where the EU has

suffered regular criticism. The agricultural subsidy early on took up 75 per cent of the EU Budget, despite generating only half that figure of GDP in the countries benefiting. The misallocation was so blatant and inefficient it only contributed to the lack of trust and confidence. The stories of warehouses across Europe to store the excessive agricultural production with wine lakes and beef mountains provided meat and drink to a sceptical media, in Britain and across Europe. The irony is reform would have come quicker, but for British farmers wanting to hold onto their subsidies.

Hardly surprising then, in the light of the failure to reform the EU and give it democratic legitimacy, that it proved singly incapable of weathering a series of storms that hit it in the five years leading up to the brutal referendum in 2016. The debt crisis of 2010–11 revealed the limitations of the euro's broad ideal of trying to meld together countries as diverse as Germany and Greece into one monetary union with one monetary policy. The discipline needed to make the flawed euro work saw Greece suffer grievously, whatever its financial excesses, at the hands of Angela Merkel's Germany.

From the summer of 2015, the influx of refugees into Greece and Italy turned European leaders against each other and made the EU appear palpably ineffective. It was easy for Eurosceptics to claim mendaciously that Syrian refugees in Germany could easily obtain EU passports and move onto the UK. The terrorist attacks in Paris and Brussels in 2015 and early 2016 were portrayed as the inevitable result of migrants coming into the EU who could not be excluded from the UK. The limitations of Schengen were cruelly exposed: the EU was unable to control either external borders or internal borders. In the words of Vernon Bogdanor, 'far from being this wicked federal superstate, the EU showed itself to be a rather incompetent, lumbering, slow-moving elephant'. The architects of Schengen, like the euro, failed to think through what was required to make it a success. The EU exacerbated the problems by failing to find the money to support the Greeks and Italians who were bearing the brunt of the migrants. Schengen may have been successful at dismantling the internal borders of those countries involved, but the devisors proved incapable of thinking through the upholding of the EU's external borders.

Member nations decided that after Delors they didn't want another weighty President of the EU Commission, so opted for a series of declining mediocrities, like Romano Prodi (1999–2004), who was admittedly stronger than his successors, José Manuel Barroso (2004–14) and Jean-Claude Juncker (2014–). The EU desperately needed figures of the same stature as Walter Hallstein (1958–67) and Roy Jenkins (1977–81). 'Jean-Claude Juncker and his kin bear a large responsibility for the rise of European populism', wrote Max Hastings, 'because they pursued profoundly anti-democratic courses and remain impenitent about doing so.' The period since 2010 has seen a revival of intergovernmental decisions – with the leaders of individual European countries, principally Merkel, becoming more important than EU figures in Brussels. This would have been fine had the national leaders in the EU been up to it. If only any had the strength and imagination of a de Gaulle or an Adenauer.

The decline in potency of the EU brought opportunities for Britain. How did Britain's leading pro-enterprise party respond to the open goal?

CHAPTER XIII

TORY IMPLOSION, 1997–2010

THE CAST:
Mr David Cameron

SUPPORTING CAST:
Mr William Hague, Mr Iain Duncan Smith,
Mr Michael Howard

ON 2 MAY 1997, after eighteen years in power, the Tories moved into opposition. The responsibility of the official opposition is to act as a government-in-waiting, to criticise the government and to offer the electorate a coherent set of policies across the piece. Opposition presented just the opportunity the Conservative Party needed – a fundamental rethink of its position on the EU – a task of renewal that is frankly difficult to achieve in power. The Conservative Party throughout its history has been the party of business, finance, wealth creation and prosperity. The EU contributed to these all very significantly. Yet successive leaders of the Conservative Party after 1997 failed to provide leadership on EU policy, and instead offered 'followship'. They were more concerned with appeasing the swelling numbers of Eurosceptics in their rank and file than coming up with a constructive pro-enterprise, open and flexible European policy, and lobbying across the EU for it to gain acceptance so it would be ready when the party was returned to power.

The Conservative Party has been the most effective political force in British history. The charge during these years is that the leaders did not act with a sufficient sense of national responsibility by failing to produce a positive policy on a fundamental area. On 19 June 1997, William Hague, who had been Welsh Secretary in Major's Cabinet, narrowly beat Ken Clarke to become party leader. The election contest was a straight fight between Eurosceptics and Europhiles. The result confirmed that 'being anything other than a Eurosceptic had become an insurmountable bar to leading the party', as author Peter Snowdon put it. Hague, at thirty-six, was the youngest Tory to lead the party since Pitt the Younger in 1783, and possessed formidable talents. But his inexperience, the divided state of the party and quality of his principal opponent,

Tony Blair, were against him. More a 'Euro-pragmatist' than a Eurosceptic, he was to become pro-EU in his later years as Foreign Secretary (2010–14).

Hague approached his task of finding a post-Major position for the Conservative Party on the EU in an incremental rather than a strategic manner. On 24 October 1997, he decided the party would not seek a referendum on the single currency during the current parliament, but would oppose membership outright, which led to resignations from his shadow Cabinet. For the 1999 European Parliament elections, he favoured a defensive position: 'In Europe, not run by Europe.' The Conservatives beat Labour, a general surprise and one of its very few successes against Blair, with 36 per cent of the vote albeit on a very low turnout of only 24 per cent. The lesson Hague and his team took away was that Euroscepticism was a winning formula, and they carried this into the general election in June 2001. It proved the second worst result for the Conservatives since 1832, just one seat gained on the near annihilation of 1997.

Conservatives do not like losing, and are far more ruthless than Labour in dispensing of their leaders when they don't bring success. The party lurched more to the Eurosceptic right in its search for Hague's successor. Three of the five candidates in the 2001 leadership election were on the right of the party. Clarke stood again, but the party had moved still more against his outlook. Iain Duncan Smith (IDS) received the enthusiastic support of Thatcher: 'I do not see how [Ken Clarke] would lead today's Conservative Party to anything other than disaster' she wrote in the *Daily Telegraph*. IDS carried the day, and spoke of ushering in a new era of success for the Conservatives. But it is always difficult for a leader to appeal for loyalty when their own record has shown anything but. IDS had succeeded Tebbit as MP for Chingford, Essex in 1992. He quickly established himself as the son of Tebbit, relentlessly defying the whip and, during the divisions over Maastricht, voting with his party on just four of sixty-two opportunities. He was the anti-EU group's head-bangers' head-banger.

IDS believed that his victory as a high priest of Euroscepticism had settled the issue in the party for good. So he tried to move the focus away from Europe and onto public services and social reform, in which he believed deeply. Blair's second defeat at the hands of Brown on the euro in 2003 had further removed the question of Britain joining from the agenda. Here was a space, when the party was relatively tranquil about Europe and before UKIP began pressing for Britain to leave, where it could have constructed a position, but it preferred to play to the press gallery, scoring debating points over long-term strategy. IDS had the opportunity, not least as a

Eurosceptic, to formulate a Conservative pro-business policy for Britain in the EU.

9/11 changed the nature of the political discourse. 'Nobody was interested in us: it was the biggest crisis to hit the western world, and nobody cared about a political party that had a new leader', IDS said later. But they might have cared if the new leader had something worthwhile to say. IDS was hopelessly ill-suited to match Blair. Support for him dwindled, culminating in a 'no-confidence' vote in October 2003 that he lost by ninety votes to seventy-five.

Michael Howard, his successor, was a much weightier figure who had been Major's Home Secretary (1993–97). Tired of leadership elections, the party chose Howard as the next leader unopposed. Where IDS had been tentative, Howard was authoritative. He appointed Eurosceptics to key positions, notably Michael Ancram as shadow Foreign Secretary and David Davis as shadow Home Secretary. The debate over the European constitution provided Howard with an opportunity to strike at Labour and whip up support among his Eurosceptic MPs and the press. He put pressure on Blair to call a referendum on the constitution, only to be disarmed when Blair announced in April 2004 that he would indeed hold one. Speaking in the Commons, Howard said it was time to 'confront' this 'unrelenting, though partially ... successful campaign to persuade Britain that Europe is a conspiracy aimed at us, rather than a partnership designed for us and others to pursue our national interests properly'.

In the European elections the following month, the Conservatives again performed better than Labour, but their share of the vote fell by 9 per cent. UKIP was on the march. In September 2004, at a by-election in Hartlepool, the Tories came fourth behind UKIP: 'the worst by-election performance by an official opposition in modern history' proclaimed the *Daily Telegraph*. Howard reacted with a reshuffle of his Cabinet that hinted at desperation: seasoned Eurosceptic John Redwood came in as shadow Deregulation Secretary.

The 2005 general election loomed; fearing a repeat of Hartlepool, Howard brought in Australian election guru Lynton Crosby to run the campaign and outwit UKIP. No coherent policy on Britain's place in Europe was offered to the electorate. Instead the party led on immigration, which contributed to anti-EU fervour. Immigration and the EU were increasingly being seen as inseparable in the eyes of the Eurosceptic press. The Conservatives performed better than expected in the general election on 6 May. Blair's majority was halved with Labour winning only 35.2 per cent of the vote – the lowest ever share for a victorious party. But the Tories' share of the vote had increased only by 0.5 per cent, and the sense was that Howard was not the man to take the party forward.

David Cameron emerged at the party conference that October as the frontrunner to succeed him. Cameron knew he would only win on a strongly Eurosceptic platform. His wildly popular speech, which saw his ratings double, criticised Blair's government for making 'promises that no one believed' and passing 'powers to a European Union that no one trusts'. His challengers from the right were David Davis and Liam Fox. Cameron opted to match the latter's commitment to withdraw Tory MPs from the European People's Party (EPP) in the European parliament. This group had consistently angered Eurosceptics in the Conservative Party by its unwavering support for the EU, even if the centre-right coalition shared many key Conservative policies. In the run-off between Cameron and Davis, the former won in October 2005 with a resounding 68 per cent of the vote.

Now as Leader of the Opposition, Cameron repeated the error of his three predecessors and dodged formulating a positive Conservative strategy on the EU. In his first conference speech as party leader in October 2006, he pressed for the party to stop 'banging on about Europe'. Some hope. The plea fell on deaf ears. His pledge to remove Tory MPs from the EPP pleased Eurosceptics but alienated European leaders, above all German Chancellor, Angela Merkel. The bad blood generated in Europe came back to haunt him as Prime Minister. He had no more success with offering a 'cast-iron guarantee' in September 2007 to hold a referendum on the Lisbon Treaty, which concluded the long discussions on the EU constitution. It was based on a calculation that was to prove false: he didn't believe that the twenty-seven EU countries would ratify Lisbon before the next general election in Britain. But when the Irish voted 'yes' on the second attempt in October 2009, the momentum accelerated, leaving just the Czech Republic to ratify the treaty, which it did in November. The treaty was now law and he was told firmly that the case could not be reopened by a British referendum on Lisbon. So Cameron had to resort to a promise that all future European treaties would be put to a referendum, and to promise a Sovereignty Bill if the Tories won the next general election to 'lock in' this supremacy of UK laws. Eurosceptics were neither pleased nor convinced. They believed they had been led up the hill with the promise of a referendum, only to be led down again empty-handed.

The repeated policy of trying to placate the Eurosceptics rather than the hard task of leadership in opposition only stored problems for the party whenever it came back to power. The die was cast.

In particular, it meant that when the time came for Cameron and his colleagues in 2016 to make a positive case for British membership of the EU – a case they should have been constructing since 2005 – it lacked all authenticity, because they had spent their political capital dissing the EU.

CHAPTER XIV

THE RISE OF NATIONALISTIC POPULISM, 2005-2016

THE CAST:

Mr Nigel Farage

SUPPORTING CAST:

Mr Enoch Powell , Mr James Goldsmith

NATIONALISM DID NOT COME out of a blue sky. We should be careful of allocating blame to British politicians for their action or inaction when there has been a global trend towards the authoritarian, closed right wing of politics. Vladimir Putin and Donald Trump may be the frontrunners, but there are plenty of examples closer to home of previously fringe elements becoming mainstream (Marine Le Pen in France, Geert Wilders in Holland) or previously respectable centre-right parties becoming illiberal nationalists (Viktor Orbán in Hungary).

That said, there were some exclusively British embarrassments and bad decisions along the way. Intimations of what was to come arose in the first Blair term, with assertive liberalism being met by a traditionalist conservative reaction. When Hague raised fears of Britain becoming a 'foreign land' in the 2001 election, he did not go on to say anything about migration, but it was heard as a dog whistle by many voters. Calling for referendums on treaties so comparatively minor as Amsterdam (1997) and Nice (2001) devalued the idea and offered bait to the more fanatical anti-EU backbenchers, suggesting that the more they pushed, the more the leadership might concede. Even before 1997, James Goldsmith's Referendum Party was used as a tool in disputes within the Conservative Party, to intimidate intra-party opponents, marking out a territory of right-wing anti-Europeanism for UKIP to colonise from its founding in 1993.

When the economic crisis hit in 2007, it was all too easy to blame immigrants for unemployment, stagnant wages and poverty, for disease even. In 2014, Nigel Farage proposed HIV-positive people should be banned from migrating to Britain, describing it as a 'good start' in controlling the UK's borders. Few did much to counter such ideas. It has never been much in the interests of British politicians or media to stand up for migrants.

The disruptive potential of the issue was initially beyond the comprehension of mainstream politicians who had been governing for a decade and seeing the benefits of the open economy. If one moment highlights this it is Gordon Brown's bafflement at being confronted with the incoherently expressed, 'bigoted' worries of Gillian Duffy in Rochdale in April 2010. Brown was far from the only leader to dismiss and misread such popular worries. Nationalist politicians always claimed that it was impossible to have a debate about immigration because of 'political correctness' but this was not true – the media was full of the issue. But too many of the arguments were circular or sensational.

A fringe xenophobic or worse element has always been present in British politics. It takes different forms at different times, and the choice for 'respectable' politics is whether to fight it or surrender, either overtly or by co-opting its central message. Consider Enoch Powell's myth-making in the 'Rivers of Blood' speech in April 1968 where, faux-innocently, he repeated stories that he said were doing the rounds among his constituents about black children racially harassing elderly white women and 'the black man having the whip hand over the white man'. Had Powell been a better man ethically, with a greater sense of his duty as a political leader, he would not have dabbled in such material. But he was roundly condemned by his party leader Edward Heath and Prime Minister Harold Wilson (not normally a politician drawn to a difficult stand on an issue), even though the public at large seemed to agree with Powell. For many Eurosceptics like Thatcher, though tellingly not all, Powell's ideological nationalism was unsavoury and deplorable.

In 2014, Nigel Farage unconsciously (or not) echoed Powell: 'It wasn't until after we got past Grove Park [a London suburb station] that I could actually hear English being audibly spoken in the carriage. Does that make me feel slightly awkward? Yes … This country, in a short space of time, has frankly become unrecognisable.' It was a sly version of what Powell was doing in Rivers of Blood. Farage is Powell's linear inheritor, but his intellectual and moral inferior; perhaps more of a Peter Griffiths, the Conservative candidate at Smethwick who defended people who had used a notorious racist slogan (though he wouldn't use it himself) on the grounds that it was an authentic expression of popular opinion in the 1964 general election. Farage himself went very close to voicing that thought:

'Any normal and fair-minded person would have a perfect right to be concerned if a group of Romanian people suddenly moved in next door.'

Farage may have regretted his choice of words, but even in doing so he also made a broad-brush comment associating Romanians with criminality. Even *The Sun* came out and criticised him: 'This is racism, pure and simple ... It IS racist to smear Romanians for being Romanian.' Contrast Farage to the Conservative MP Anna Soubry, who remembered that it is a duty of political leadership to tell the truth and challenge ignorance and laziness. During the referendum campaign, she recalled in a *Guardian* interview a man she had met in the East Midlands who had told her that you no longer hear anyone speaking English in Newark.

I thought, 'I've had enough of this.' I looked him straight in the eye and said: 'That is crap and you know it. I know Newark, and that's crap. Of course you hear people speaking English! Overwhelmingly they're speaking English in Newark.' And you could see him thinking, 'that's absolutely true...' Well of course it's true! But it's become acceptable to say that, and people weren't being challenged. So I challenged him.'

Where does Farage stand in our story here? Is he one of the fifteen guilty men? It is one of the great philosophical questions. Who is more guilty – the fanatic or the liar? Is genuinely believing in something an adequate defence, or is the true believer actually worse? One cannot fail to recognise that to Farage, his opposition to the EU and immigration is a sincere, mutually consistent belief system. There are reasons why one might want to acquit Farage of some charges, because he believes deeply in his cause and believes he's done a great public service, while convict Boris Johnson for his opportunism and dilettantism.

Is Farage off the hook? No. The believer compromises the integrity of his campaign when he adopts methods that involve deceits or distortions in pursuit of what he thinks is the greater good, or evoking and exploiting the darker side of human nature. Farage, like Powell, has done this, but Powell would never have embraced irrationality and anti-intellectualism so overtly. Powell also had the restraint not to gloat in public. He celebrated Heath's defeat in 1974 in private, humming the *Te Deum* to himself when he saw the news. Ugly triumphalism was not for him.

The Farage mask of faux affable bloke slipped dramatically within hours of the referendum result. First there was his claiming the result as a victory for the 'ordinary, decent' people, marking out 48 per cent of the voters (and all the resident EU citizens who could not vote) presumably as not ordinary, not decent, not proper people. Farage's announcement that Brexit had been accomplished 'without a shot being fired' was what can only be mildly put as crass and tasteless in the light of the murder less than a week before of Jo Cox by a far-right terrorist. Farage followed this up in December by baselessly accusing Cox's widower, Brendan, of associating with extremists.

The day after the referendum, Farage issued a blanket condemnation of his fellow MEPs, without a shred of dignity or magnanimity. It was they, apparently, who had never had a proper job, according to this professional politician, minor financial sector drone and permanent fixture on the British media circuit. Gloating and hubris hardly seem sufficient charges. So much for the sentiment of the great inspirer of the Dunkirk spirit, Winston Churchill: 'In victory, magnanimity!'

Having inveighed against the evils of foreigners expressing their views on the British referendum, Farage promptly turned around and started singing the praises of Donald Trump and Marine Le Pen. 'That Obama creature – a loathsome individual who couldn't stand our country,' was a strangely emphatic thing to say about the mild-mannered, professorial President whose eight-year administration had been notably devoid of scandal. One wonders quite which personal characteristic of Obama might have triggered such a visceral response from Farage.

Farage gave a warm endorsement, printed as a comment

piece in the *Daily Telegraph*, of Marine Le Pen, a woman whom the French courts have ruled as acceptably described as a fascist. She was 'the best candidate for Brexit Britain' and the tragedy is that for once, Farage may have been entirely correct and honest. Brexit has put the UK on the side of the outlaws and wreckers of the world, from Trump to the murderous President Duterte of the Philippines, to the heirs of Pétain and Laval who arouse such warm feelings in Farage's breast. It is necessary, but also not sufficient, to lay some blame for this predicament at the door of Farage and his fellow nationalists.

And do Farage and his ilk feel a glimmer of doubt about what they have done to Britain, and how they did it? On 16 September 2016, Farage went for a celebratory skinny dip with Arron Banks, the businessman who gave UKIP £1 million and the Leave campaign £7.5 million. When questioned about alleged irregularities in the referendum campaign, he said: '[We] pushed the boundary of everything, right to the edge … no one cares!'

No one cares? We care.

CHAPTER XV

MULTIPLE REFERENDUM ERRORS, 2013–2016

THE CAST:

Mr David Cameron

SUPPORTING CAST:

Mr George Osborne, the hardened anti-EU Tory MPs
and press

AS THE MONTHS OF coalition government after 2010
ground on, Cameron became increasingly aware that the ethos
of compromise it required could not contain the frothing
anti-EU MPs in the party. The fateful decision to promise an
'in-out' referendum came in his Bloomberg speech on 23 January 2013. In the face of the intense pressure he was under from
his own party and from UKIP nationally and from the country
(as seen in the 1 million signature petition for a referendum) it

would have required huge reserves of statesmanship to have avoided calling it. He failed, but it was a high hurdle to leap, and whether any Prime Ministers in history would have acted differently is a moot point.

Cameron, with all the confidence of his youth, was a gambler. Michael Gove described him as 'the kind of poker player who waits and reads the other players and bets when he knows the alignment is in his favour'. Even in retrospect, Cameron considers: 'I thought it right to hold the referendum because this issue had been poisoning British politics for years.' This is a revealing comment. Had this issue been poisoning British politics for years? It had certainly become increasingly acrid with the stellar rise of UKIP. In an interview with the *Financial Times* in March 2015, the interviewer recounted:

> Mr Cameron says he hopes to be remembered as the prime minister who resolves the country's two existential questions in the first part of the twenty-first century. One is, does the United Kingdom want to stay together? Yes. Secondly, does the United Kingdom want to stay in a reformed European Union? Yes.

Cameron had not just the nation but the cohesion of the Conservative Party firmly in his sights.

But there is little evidence that voters thought very much about the subject or regarded it as important as the Westminster-bubble politicians did. On the eve of the fateful Bloomberg speech, just 6 per cent of voters were listing Europe as one of the most important issues facing Britain. In January 2015, 2 per cent thought Europe was the most important issue, and only 9 per cent thought it was in the top two concerns according to Ipsos MORI. The voters were much more concerned about immigration, the economy, the NHS and poverty and inequality.

The area of British politics that the Europe issue had been poisoning for years was specifically the Conservative Party. It was deeply divided, albeit less between moderate pro- and anti-Europeans. The pragmatists on each side had called a truce and were prepared to live with the current state of European integration but not concede any more – a position conceded under the coalition by the 'referendum lock' to call a referendum on any future changes. But the extreme anti-European elements in the Conservative Party would simply not stop banging on about Europe. Doing so was a convenient lever to exert pressure on Cameron, a leader they never liked and whose modernising instincts on same-sex marriage they detested, and whom they blamed for not getting a majority in the 2010 general election. The rise of UKIP in the polls from the end of 2012 only added to the pressure and its leverage. The anti-EU right has always had a double role, as competitors for the votes, but also an alliance with the press enabling them to bend the Tory leadership to their will.

Conceding the referendum was consistent with Cameron's past means of dealing with the anti-EU right wing – leaving the European People's Party and making the promise of a referendum on the Treaty of Lisbon. It would solve a problem for the moment, and Cameron had sufficient confidence in his own wiliness that he would be able to manoeuvre his way out of future problems. George Osborne had a keener sense of the limits of political cleverness and thought the whole thing was a bad idea. Even in the short term, it failed to see off UKIP, who continued to make big gains in local elections, by-elections and the European Parliament elections in 2014 even after the referendum was announced. But once its decision had been taken, Osborne was the most red-blooded of Cameron's team fighting the referendum on 'belligerence-max'. They had won the Scottish referendum in September 2014 in this way: it would work for this one too.

Calling a referendum on Europe was to prove to be a way of crystallising all the subjects that people cared more about – immigration, inequality, stretched public services, the general sense of being adrift in a world that does not care or understand – into a debate that was supposedly about Europe but had little to do with the realities and policies of the European Union. The most powerful weapon of leadership is to shape the agenda, determine which topics are discussed and in which terms. By conceding the referendum Cameron handed over this power, post-dated, to the anti-Europeans. It ushered in a period of national life in which all the discontents and problems facing Britain would be discussed as if 'Europe' were central and even responsible for all of them.

How did this happen? With hindsight, it was hardly surprising when for years British politicians had been shifting the blame for all sorts of ills to 'Europe'. Labour figures had done this too, but they had been out of power since 2010. 'Having spent two decades striking poses as Eurosceptics to curry favour with their party [the Conservatives] they believed that they could change their tune in the last second of the eleventh hour in the referendum,' as Nick Clegg put it. Even Juncker broadly agreed, saying in the German press: 'If someone complains about Europe from Monday to Saturday then nobody is going to believe him on Sunday when he says he is a convinced European.'

The other massive strategic miscalculation in calling the referendum was in failing to contextualise the vote. At the time, it seemed a good chance that framing it as a once-and-for-all, sudden-death majority verdict, would be the best chance of shutting down the debate within the Tory Party. It might have been, but history shows us that people arguing for a change they believe in (whether withdrawal from Europe or Scottish independence) are rarely silenced by losing a referendum. The government might have taken notice that it is usual for radical constitutional change to need more than a bare '50 per cent plus' one of those voting in a referendum. Wrenching change requires a settled will and general consent, not a narrow margin on the quick. Other referendums, including the Scottish referendum of 1979, have not been based on a simple majority alone: they have required either minimum shares of the whole electorate or consent from a majority of the territorial units that comprise the state. An opportunity at the start to build in such features was not taken. Official recognition could have been obtained that a verdict of, say, 45–55 either way would not close the issue, and would mean that Britain would return to negotiations with the aim of getting a better deal. But no. The relentless 'yes–no' juggernaut drove forward, its drivers confident of coming in first. They were anxious to move on. They had a whole agenda to execute.

Cameron made two other linked errors in his approach to the referendum. The first, the management of the renegotiation process with Brussels. It was inadequately thought through;

not until late did the UK state its objectives, and these turned out to be modest by the standards that had been allowed to form in people's minds. For raising expectations, he must take some blame: he told conference delegates in October 2014 about immigration: 'Britain, I know you want this sorted so I will go to Brussels, I will not take no for an answer and when it comes to free movement – I will get what Britain needs!' The expectations of a much better deal may have been unreasonable, but were not doused down sufficiently. The February 2016 agreement in Brussels in fact gave Cameron a fair amount of what he asked for under each of his headings, even ones that had looked difficult. The press predictably trashed it. They were always going to, even if Cameron had achieved a deal that made Norman Tebbit shout out 'yes, yes, yes!'

The renegotiation took place too quickly. This was only partly Cameron's fault, because the rest of the EU had other business on its agenda as well, and for political reasons all the participants were keen to get the UK–EU agreement sorted out. Everyone was in a hurry. Previous Prime Ministers, notably John Major, had done their homework – studying the issues, building diplomatic alliances, playing the game of four-dimensional chess – before major European agreements. Cameron tried harder than many saw behind the scenes, but the mood in Europe was against him. He gave the impression to Europeans from the text of the Bloomberg speech onwards that he was looking for something he could say 'yes' to, even though he had to pretend otherwise, which diminished his leverage in Brussels. Unlike Wilson in 1975, he did not keep his cards close to his chest. The renegotiation process was not taken seriously enough either by the EU in general or the UK, to offer something that could be convincingly presented as a fresh start for Britain. It was an opportunity lost.

Cameron had to feign preparedness to recommend a 'Leave' vote if the negotiations failed, at least between May 2015 and February 2016. He said several times that the UK would be fine if it did leave the EU, which undercut his later pro-EU campaign credentials. It was a contorted and unconvincing pose and legitimised the idea of leaving. How could he argue in a campaign that it was vital for the national interest to vote Remain while a few months earlier he was (ostensibly) prepared to recommend Leave?

There was no very good reason why the vote had to happen in June 2016. He could have told EU leaders in February 2016 the offer was not good enough. Think again. The referendum did not need to happen until mid-2017. But his team thought they had secured enough; they wanted to be rid of the damned issue and were overconfident about winning. They were on an express train that was hurtling forward and which had no time to make stops. No time for a pause, no time for reflection. It was a gamble for high stakes that went horrifically wrong. Andrew Marr wrote how 'without a much tougher curb on migrant numbers he was likely to lose the referendum. From his perspective, he really did need to push the German Chancellor much harder. The consequences of that error could hardly have been bigger.' A more considered leader would have bought some time. The Remain campaign, particularly the Conservative Remainers, needed it to organise and argue; they had been artificially delayed and held back by Cameron's necessary ambivalence before the February agreement while the Leavers had been building their double-headed campaign machine apace.

The timetable left a perilously narrow window between signing the agreement and the beginning of the campaign. Moving the vote that much further away from the 2015 migration crisis in Europe would have helped, as would a further period of stable economic growth. It would have helped too if Cameron and Osborne had taken action more directly on the issues that the voters were really worried about, particularly job insecurity, low pay and migration, and its impact of cuts on those more deprived areas which felt most excluded from the country's economic success story.

Cameron hoped to take the poison out of the issue within

the Conservative Party, and allow the country to move on to a more positive relationship with the EU. This was not an unworthy ambition. Had the vote been won, he would have been a key figure remodelling the EU and his country. He had extensive plans to build a more prosperous and fairer country. He could have become the hero of the story. Unlike many of the star guilty men of 2016, and of 1940, he was a decent and honourable man. But history will cast him as the scapegoat, and possibly the villain of the story.

For all that, the referendum could still have been won. There was nothing inevitable about the result. The media could just have tipped the balance either way.

CHAPTER XVI

THE FOAMING OF THE PRESS BARONS, 2015–2016

THE CAST:

Mr Paul Dacre, Mr Rupert Murdoch

SUPPORTING CAST:

Mr Richard Desmond

YEARS OF METICULOUS HARD work by Paul Dacre and Rupert Murdoch, as well as by a host of other powerful press figures such as Conrad Black, the Barclay brothers and Richard Desmond, all came home to roost in the referendum campaign. They revelled in the Leave result on 23 June 2016. It is what they had worked towards and yearned for over many years.

The contrast with the 1975 referendum, when almost all the press titles were in favour of remaining in Europe, was stark.

In 2016, only *The Guardian*, the *Financial Times*, *The Times* (but not the *Sunday Times*), the *Mail on Sunday* and the *Daily Mirror* supported remain. A University of Loughborough study found an 82 per cent circulation advantage in favour of Brexit. A Reuters Institute survey of the national press coverage in the campaign found that it was 'heavily skewed in favour of Brexit'.

The referendum was indeed the most important democratic vote in British history. The electorate deserved truth, not innuendo. Did they receive it? 'EXCLUSIVE: BOMB-SHELL CLAIM OVER EUROPE VOTE. QUEEN BACKS BREXIT. EU going in wrong direction, she says', proclaimed *The Sun* on 9 March 2016, a claim based on anonymous sources which the Independent Press Standards Organisation (IPSO) declared 'significantly misleading'. The editor of *The Sun* rejected the ruling and thirteen days later a new headline appeared: 'WHAT QUEEN ASKED DINNER GUESTS: GIVE ME 3 GOOD REASONS TO STAY IN EUROPE. Sorry Ma'am, we can't think of ONE'. The Queen has been meticulous during her 65-year reign in not expressing her personal views; much of her authority has derived from that very fact. To have politicised her at such a volatile time for the nation, was an act of considerable irresponsibility. Less blame-worthy was the argument *The Sun* used ten days from polling day: 'We urge our readers to beLEAVE in Britain and vote to quit the EU on June 23'. The paper then offered its views on the net impact of the EU on Britain: 'We must set ourselves free from dictatorial Brussels. Throughout our 43-year membership of the European Union it has proved increasingly greedy, wasteful, bullying and breathtakingly incompetent in a crisis.'

The *Mail* did as much as any paper to destroy credibility in the February renegotiations. Its front page asked 'Who will speak for England?' The phrase had been used against Chamberlain, posing Cameron as his modern day equivalent. 'As in 1939, we are at a crossroads in our island's history,' it said. Cato would have pointed out that in 1939 the paper was sympathetic to fascism.

The Mail Online announced on 17 February 2016: 'Criminal convictions for EU migrants leap by 40% in five years: 700 found guilty every week in the UK'. It published a correction in March, stating the figures related to 'notifications' not 'convictions'. The next month, the Mail Online stated: 'Report shows the NHS is nearly at breaking point as massive influx of EU migrants forces doctors to take on 1.5 million extra patients in just three years.' The statement was widely disputed and at best a gross distortion. On 15 June, the front-page headline in the *Daily Mail* declared: 'As politicians squabble over border controls, yet another lorry load of migrants arrives in the UK declaring ... WE'RE FROM EUROPE – LET US IN!' The paper had to issue a correction to the article as it was made clear that the migrants in the video were not from Europe at all, but Iraq and Kuwait.

Katie Hopkins was one of the Mail Online's principal columnists pouring out a stream of invective against the EU. On 24 June her jubilant article carried the headline: 'Pinch me, I must be dreaming. It's the day Britain stood up proud and tall and reclaimed its birth right'. She told her readers this was the day:

> We decided to stop paying bureaucrats simply for turning up, to reject the dictatorship of Junker [*sic*] and his crony mates telling us to stand in line, and send Obama to the back a queue [*sic*] for his pension cheque.
>
> We stood up for our own families, who need doctors [*sic*] appointments and primary schools for their kids, who did not deserve to be put in second place behind families fresh off a plane. We voted to stop sending your taxes back to kids in countries other than our own.

Immigration was referred to extensively in the campaign. A King's College London report in May 2017 cited over 4,000 online articles during the campaign discussing immigration, significantly more than those published on health, education and housing. References to immigration tripled over the course of the campaign, especially after 'purdah' began on 27 May, which meant that there could be no official rebuttals to these extravagant claims. *The Mail* led on immigration on seventeen of the final twenty-three days leading up to the referendum.

Migrants were blamed for everything, from creating a housing crisis by the *Daily Mail*, 19 May 2016, 'MIGRANTS SPARK HOUSING CRISIS: Now EU tells Britain to build more homes as open borders send population soaring'; to stealing British benefits, as in the *Express*, 24 March 2016: 'EU migrants pocket MORE tax credits cash and child benefits than BRITISH workers'; to swamping NHS maternity services and taking primary school places in the *Daily Telegraph* on 6 May. They were blamed for bringing diseases into Britain and importing organised crime as in the *Express*: 'Top police chief: EU "free movement" allows criminals to come to UK and FLOURISH. THE European Union's open borders policy has allowed Islamist terrorists to roam the streets of the Continent at will'.

Certain nationalities were singled out by the press, particularly Turks and Albanians, but also Poles and Romanians. As noted by Martin Moore and Gordon Ramsay of King's

College, the language used to describe migration was hyperbolic and hysterical, drawing upon the vocabulary for 'natural disasters (flooding, swamped), animals and insects (flocking, stampeding, swarming) or foreign attack (invaders, storming, besieged)'. Priti Patel, the current International Development Secretary, claimed migrants were taking up primary school places, making the accusation on the day that parents received letters about their children's places in primary school. Given the timing, it surely could only have fed resentment, heightened emotion and maximised impact?

Moore and Ramsay found that 100 per cent of evaluative mentions of Albanians were negative, compared to 98 per cent of mentions about Turks. The great majority of these were made by *The Sun*, the *Daily Mail* and the *Express*. Association of these migrants with crime and violence was common. Front pages explicitly featured foreign murderers and rapists, decontextualising the findings, making them difficult to verify. Photographs were regularly used in a highly emotive way: an article in the *Express* about foreign criminals used a stock photograph of someone at night-time standing over a body, pointing at it with a gun. Focus groups for the Leave campaign found early on that Turkey was a red-flag subject for many voters. The suggestion that Turks were coming freely to Britain was hammered home in the press.

Ten years earlier, *The Sun* sold twice as many copies than it does now, with a print circulation of over 3 million now reduced to just over 1.5 million. The *Mail*'s loss of paper copies for the has been compensated by its very significant online following, with the website's news content bolstered by photographs of showbiz personalities and scantily clad women. The titles may not be as key in the formation of national opinion as they were as recently as the 1990s. Successive surveys nevertheless show a strong correlation between press readership and voting patterns, it can be in part explained by voters of a particular persuasion choosing the title that most conforms with their own outlook.

Decades of negative reporting on the EU since the 1980s, with little rebuttal or political leadership from the top putting a positive case, had an inevitable impact in forming perceptions of the EU during the campaign. It was the long-term impact of these stories, rather than lurid headlines during the actual campaign itself, which was primarily responsible for moulding public opinion.

The impact of the press would not have had the credence it did without the BBC, to an extent which the BBC has still not fully acknowledged. The British public maintains huge levels of trust in the BBC. Surveys show it to be consistently and by a considerable margin the most relied upon outlet for news, with ITV and Sky doing well, but less trusted. But the BBC's news reports are very significantly led by newspaper titles, in part because it is legally bound to be impartial. Unable to set its own agenda, it borrows it from the press. BBC Radio 4's *Today* programme sets the agenda for the BBC throughout the day. 'The degree to which the BBC took as public opinion the views of right-wing newspapers was shocking', says Brian Cathcart. Steven Barnett points out that the BBC was in the final stages of a Charter review period during the referendum campaign and became 'obsessed with balancing every single argument, even the most patently absurd ... its coverage was much more inclined to follow rather than lead'. The *Daily Mail* and *The Sun* would bang on about the Turks pouring into Europe, and the BBC would then bang on about it. Even if some BBC content challenged what the papers were saying about Turks, they were still talking about Turks, which is exactly what the Leavers wanted. This agenda-setting is now the principal power of the *Daily Mail* and *The Sun*, and the *Daily Express* too, Cathcart says.

Social media played a core part in the 2016 referendum, another clear difference with 1975. Martin Moore believes it was 'very significant' in enabling Leave to win. Dominic Cummings, the ferociously single-minded campaign director for Vote Leave, said that Leave spent 98 per cent of its money on digital media, especially Facebook, with messaging on users' feeds tweaked to respond to specific concerns voters had. The laws around referendums are balefully out of date and have not yet responded to developments on social media, another failure of electoral law during the campaign.

Leave.EU claimed it reached as many as 15 million voters in some weeks of the campaign. One video was viewed 9.3 million times on Facebook. Analysis suggests, if not conclusively, that voters targeted by Leave.EU turned out in disproportionately high numbers. Martin Fletcher of the *New Statesman* argued that Leave.EU's social media strategy and Farage's rallies 'combined to connect with a large chunk of the blue-collar vote which ultimately proved absolutely critical to the result'. Videos on Leave.EU's Facebook page included titles such as: 'Are you concerned about the amount of crime being committed in the UK by foreign criminals?', which ended with the message: 'Isn't it time to take back control?'. Another video on the Facebook page asked: 'Are you worried about the overcrowding of the UK and the burden on the NHS?' Leave.EU's tweet said: 'Islamic extremism is a real threat to our way of life. Act now before we see an Orlando-style atrocity here'.

The media in all its forms carried the day for Leave. Dacre and Murdoch and their fellow travellers can feel very proud of what they achieved.

Does it trouble them that their victory was won through deceit and manipulation? Perhaps. But they have their prize. Power. Profits.

What profits a man if he gains the whole world but loses his own soul?

CHAPTER XVII

CAMPAIGN FOLLIES, FEBRUARY–JUNE 2016

THE CAST:
Mr David Cameron

SUPPORTING CAST:
Mr George Osborne

THE GROUNDWORK FOR THE Remain case had been poorly laid: principally Cameron's responsibility. But the referendum could still have been won if the Remainers had fought a half-decent case. The guilty party here, unequivocally, is George Osborne. Having opposed the referendum at the outset, warning Cameron, 'there is a good chance we will lose', he is absolved of being one of the main fifteen guilty men. But it was Osborne who then provided the single-minded, win-at-any-costs strategy, just as he had done on the Alternative Vote referendum campaign in May 2011 with its 'fuck everyone else' strategy. So too did he come to grip the referendum campaign by the balls. Only, on this occasion, his testicular clench emasculated the patient, leaving it fighting for life on the operating table.

Three major strategic errors lost Remain the referendum: the wrong message, the wrong people and the wrong tactics. To Andrew Marr, it was 'the biggest establishment cock-up in my lifetime'.

Here was a triple-A textbook example of negative psychology. There are only two outcomes with negativity: you either lose badly or you win badly. Either way, trust is the casualty. Rather than taking the high ground by giving an optimistic picture of the benefits of the EU, treating opponents and their arguments respectfully, reassuring those who felt alienated from Westminster and behaving like statesmen, the (male-dominated) strategy was awash with nastiness and negativity. 'We need more fear. Fear is the only thing can win it for us ... We need lots of fear. We need as much fear as we can get,' admitted one of the Cameron–Osborne team.

How did they make this terrible mistake? Because fear was believed to be responsible for the Scottish referendum victory in May 2014, and again for the surprise general election victory in May 2015. They let themselves be convinced by their pollsters that they would win, and that the electorate's fears over the economy would always trump fears over immigration. Trying to persuade voters to love the EU and see it positively was an utter waste of time, they let themselves believe, especially given the disobliging comments on the EU uttered by Cameron and Osborne over the years.

What other pitch might they have made? At the heart of the campaign, as some urged them, should have been Britain's transition from 'the sick man of Europe' to the world's most respected soft power and its fifth biggest economy. The electorate could have been presented with a choice: build on that momentum, or risk jeopardising it. Remainers could have spoken about Europe being at peace since the creation of the EU, and the spread of rights, democracy and tolerance under it. Voters could have been offered a vision of multiple identities: English/Scottish/Irish/Welsh, British *and* European. To combat the impression of an EU behemoth, Remainers could have explained that in most key policy areas including education, health and housing, the EU makes little or no impact. To argue the EU ran great swathes of British life was utter nonsense.

To combat the untruth that Britain has been powerless within the EU, the electorate needed reminders of the many gains that Britain has secured within it, including freer trade and employment rights. Or more recently, how Britain has led the EU in securing a digital single market and energy union, with benefits in security and fuel pricing for all. Remainers could have spelled out the EU's role in ensuring cheaper mobile data roaming charges across Europe, and in helping make affordable, safe, airline travel available for all. Or they could have championed how the EU has increased jobs and trade and given people of all ages opportunities across Europe. Critically, they should have acknowledged immigration as a problem, but made clear this was not exclusively the fault of the EU, worked to achieve a temporary cap and provided reassurance on future measures.

Charles Grant of the Centre for European Reform was one of many who plied No. 10 with messages, saying: 'Don't focus only on the economic costs of leaving the EU. Younger people, in particular, want to hear positive reasons for staying in – they want more vision and fewer economic statistics.' No. 10's response was the repeatedly made promise that a positive message would be coming and that young people would be offered a vision. But this vision never came. The referendum was won by Leave because vast numbers of the left-behinds in ex-industrial towns, in the midlands and in the north, were sick of years of unfulfilled promises and of seeing their living standards stagnate, or worse: a condition they attributed, not always incorrectly, to migration.

No one, not even Cameron, was going to change tack. There was no Plan B on the referendum any more than for austerity.

So Osborne hit out in April with the Treasury-backed claim that Brexit would leave the average household £4,300 worse off. His statistic almost certainly did more harm than good. The economic analysis may have been well-grounded, but it failed to convince the public, and, when supplemented by further forecasts of doom and gloom, it laid the ground all too easily for Leave to brand the whole Remain campaign as scare-mongering and 'Project Fear'. Messages came back to No. 10 that the tactic wasn't working, but like a First World War general, it ploughed on with the strategy regardless. The lesson absorbed from Bill Clinton's strategy which won him the US presidency twice in the 1990s was to differentiate on matters of the economy, produce expert opinion that bolstered your argument, and ram it down the electorate's throat.

Osborne's emergency Budget plans, announced just eleven days out from polling day, showed he had learnt nothing. The Budget threatened a £15 billion tax rise and big cuts to spending in health, education and defence if Britain voted to leave the EU. It was madness. The Budget was labelled 'George's dodgy dossier', neatly equating him with Blair and his Iraq dossier. The more worried they became that the vote would be lost, the more negativity they piled on. 'The definition of insanity is doing the same thing over and over again, but expecting different results', Einstein is supposed to have said.

The result was predictable. The Remain side sacrificed the high ground, failed to inspire the young (and not-so-young) to vote and legitimised Leave's half-truths by giving currency to the idea that 'both sides are as bad as each other'. The strategy ultimately failed to bring out the EU's core supporters in sufficient numbers, while winning over far too few of those who were undecided.

Failing to utilise their human assets was Remain's second fatal error. Too much faith was placed upon establishment voices. As Marr wrote, 'those running the Remain campaign always believed in "Project Fear"; that a barrage of warnings by the Treasury, big business, banks and international organisations would simply terrify ordinary voters – workers and pensioners alike – and pulverise the arguments for leaving.' 'The IMF is right – leaving the EU would pose major risks for the economy', tweeted Cameron in February 2016. But the public did not care for the IMF, if they even knew what it was. President Obama was going to be one of Remain's secret weapons. Much store was set by his visit to the UK in April. But his statement that Britain would 'be back of the queue' for a trade deal was resented and almost certainly backfired. It was a gift for Daniel Hannan to caricature such overtures as desperation: 'They campaigned ... chiefly through letters by hoary-headed grandees in *The Times* saying we are ordering you little people to vote Remain, to support our income.'

The Remain campaign was a pale shadow of the slick, brutal, managerial efficiency of the Leave side. They failed to make the most of Jim Messina, Obama's campaign guru, who had helped win the 2015 general election for the Conservatives. Cameron became the face of the campaign, in contrast to the multi-party Remain leadership in 1975, which featured heavyweights like Heath, Jenkins and Liberal leader Thorpe. The focus on Cameron made it too much of a referendum on his leadership, especially as he epitomised the Eton–Oxford upper-class establishment that many of the excluded so despised. His approval rating in April, two months from polling day, was even lower than Corbyn's at -24; Osborne's was even worse at -41. Cameron, damaged by the Panama Papers scandal, dwelt on by the press on the eve of the campaign, never came close to getting into his stride: no matter that he was absolved of personal blame and that the issue had nothing to do with the EU. Popular politicians were not utilised, or were brought in too late in the day, such as Scottish Conservative leader Ruth Davidson and freshly elected London Mayor Sadiq Khan, who both took part in the final debate on 22 June. Former Labour minister Alan Johnson, one of the most popular politicians in Britain, was barely utilised, while Gordon

Brown, with his powerful appeal to Scotland and Labour's heartlands, was only wheeled in late in the day. Nick Clegg was largely invisible.

Wrong tactics was the third and final failing. Despite five years of guerrilla warfare from Tory MPs during the coalition government, and twenty-five years of it since the Maastricht debates in the early 1990s, Cameron's team still seemed to believe that respect for the PM and his victory in the 2015 general election would keep the majority of MPs in line, including Gove and Johnson, and reduce rebel backbenchers to a manageable fifty or sixty. Some hope. Careful canvassing by formidable Tory MP Steve Baker pushed the number of rebels up to over 140, well beyond the comfort zone. Baker was again in action, complaining to the Electoral Commission that the original referendum question – 'Yes v. No' – was loaded, as a 'Yes' vote would appear inherently more attractive to the unde-cided. He and his allies won the day, and the vote was changed to 'Leave v. Remain'. Polls indicated that it might have been worth 4 per cent to the Leave campaign, precisely the margin of victory. Earlier tactical mistakes included accepting the period of official government, purdah, which restrained what could be published, while allowing government ministers to back Leave but remain members of government.

Labour and the Lib Dems argued that sixteen- and

seventeen-year-olds should be allowed to vote, a proposal
Cameron's team rejected allegedly because it could hurt the
Conservatives in future elections, though, as in 1975, No. 10
argued the voting age should remain the same as for parliamentary elections as a matter of consistent enfranchisement.
Remainers later calculated that the decision cost them
650,000 votes. The precise figure is unknowable, but had an
appeal been made to the young during the campaign, who felt
alienated by older voters 'taking away their future', it could
have been worth far more votes. Remain's underpowered and
disjointed tactics were weakened further by their pollsters
underestimating the large numbers of traditional non-voters
who were fired up by the Brexit side to vote Leave. This faux-
optimism militated against any change of strategy to appeal
far more to the dispossessed. As one member of the team told
Tim Shipman: 'Frankly we'd have been better off having no
polling at all.' Turnout in three major Remain areas – London,
Scotland and Northern Ireland – was lower in every Leave are
bar one.

Project Fear had pumped out so much terror into the
political bloodstream that it ended up mesmerising its own
leadership. They failed to see that the biggest fear they had to
address was the one staring them in the face from the very start
– immigration. Failure to tackle it during the campaign, and the

belief that by not talking about it, it would go away, was one of the great tactical follies. Peter Mandelson and Britain Stronger in Europe director, Will Straw, were two figures pressing Cameron to make a 'vow' telling the electorate that he'd listen to their concerns on immigration and take action to secure an emergency brake on numbers. In a critical meeting, eleven days before polling day, they pressed their case. Cameron took the point. But following a conversation with Angela Merkel, he refused to budge. By this stage his head was spinning. Sometimes in the life of No. 10, if rarely, events are just so big that the incumbents are overwhelmed by them and fail to act rationally.

The tragedy was that Cameron was a bigger man than he showed the world in the campaign. But he was neither sufficiently reflective, experienced nor perhaps mature enough to trust his own deep instincts, and prevent himself being swayed by those around him to act in a way that deep down he must have known was flawed.

He was unlucky too: he did not foresee the Syrian refugee crisis, easily confused with internal EU immigration, nor the defections of Gove and Johnson nor the limp leadership from Labour's leader. Cameron had been the youngest Prime Minister in 198 years. His curse is that as the youngest former premier since Pitt the Younger, not yet fifty when he quit, he will have years and years of life ahead to reflect on what might have been.

CHAPTER XVIII

CAMPAIGN DECEITS AND DISTORTIONS, 2015-2016

THE CAST:

Mr Dominic Cummings, Mr Boris Johnson,
Mr Nigel Farage, Mr Arron Banks

SUPPORTING CAST:

Mr Michael Gove

THE REMAIN SIDE LOST the campaign. Leave won it. But did their ends justify their means? The literature on the referendum, including Tim Shipman's seminal *All Out War*, tends to suggest both sides were as bad as the other. But is that true?

The major historic significance of the referendum, the passions on each side (much greater than for most general elections) and the high possibility of a close result, demanded a very tightly supervised campaign. Especially so because, with referendums, there is sparse accountability afterwards. The organisations that fight referendum campaigns, unlike political parties, dissolve into the Friday morning mist. They do not have to face the consequences of their transgressions. Such knowledge can contribute to a scorched-earth approach to standards of campaigning, in terms of honesty, compliance with financial and legal regulations, and encourage a blasé attitude to the making of promises and threats. A campaign can promise unicorns and then disappear, leaving some-one else with the responsibility either for producing some beasts with single spiralling horns or falling foul of the will of the people.

Nor does a referendum campaign encourage the making of promises which are mutually consistent. Extra funding for the NHS, more subsidies to farming, higher education support – these are all just suggestions you understand, and unlike a general election there is no way of punishing the parties who fail to deliver on them. And is there guilt or shame among those who pushed these promises that were not, apparently, promises at all? Are there unicorns? It was only promises, mere words. What did you expect?

Leave.EU was the baby of Nigel Farage and the businessman

Arron Banks, who had previously been a Conservative donor but who switched to UKIP in 2014 and who claimed to donate a critical £7.5 million to the Brexit campaign between 2015–2016, mostly to Leave.EU. Its propaganda was not subtle, reflecting Banks's resolute style: 'Dave wants to give 75m Turks access to your #NHS!' It distributed a video, viewed 1.6 million times, entitled: 'Are you concerned about the amount of crime being committed in the UK by foreign criminals?', ending with the message: 'Isn't it time to take back control.' Banks continued in a similar vein after the result, admitting that 'politics is a dirty business', and his cheerful blatancy has increasingly been emulated by Farage. Leave.EU's messaging was far-reaching, with Facebook and Twitter central to its potency.

Vote Leave and Leave.EU deliberately constructed themselves as opponents, refusing to share platforms and consistently insulting one another. This oppositional image was deliberate – they could launch a two-pronged attack, targeting Middle England and UKIP voters simultaneously. But despite this seeming animosity, Carole Cadwalladr wrote in *The Observer* about the cooperation between the Vote Leave and Leave.EU campaigns. *The Observer* claimed that the two data analytics firms employed by the campaigns – AggregateIQ

(Vote Leave) and the company behind Cambridge Analytica (Leave.EU) – signed an intellectual property agreement to enable the sharing of data. This covert offshore cooperation, though the allegations were contested by the companies, was described to *The Observer* by electoral law expert, Gavin Millar QC, as 'about as serious a breach of the funding rules as one can imagine in the twenty-first century'. Cambridge Analytica is owned by American billionaire Robert Mercer, who is friends with Donald Trump and Farage. During the election Mercer 'gift[ed]' the company's services to Leave. EU. And at the helm of Cambridge Analytica? Stephen Bannon – creator of 'alt-right' (some say verging on white supremacist) website Breitbart.

Compared to Leave.EU and Grassroots Out (GO), Vote Leave looked almost respectable and centrist, and it could also look the other way and tut-tut while Farage and Banks said things that the official campaign could not. Like an Ian Fleming villain, stroking a white cat, it could proclaim: 'Myself, Mr Bond, I abhor violence. But my associates may not be so scrupulous.' No doubt there was genuine bad blood and mutual contempt between them, but in practice the duality and deniability of the two Leave campaigns served their shared objective.

The Vote Leave campaign disdained Farage and vice versa.

Its supremo, Dominic Cummings, may believe that a Farage-style campaign would have lost the referendum badly and he may be right. The official voice of Vote Leave was a persuasive and clever one, blending some dark emotions, 'Australian (white country) points system' and hordes of Turks, with the more rational mechanisms of minimising people's risk aversion and the promise of a better life for all. By whipping up the immigration issue, Leave.EU and Banks provided the visceral pull towards Leave that attracted so many people who had not voted for years, and who ultimately tipped the balance.

We should not absolve the official Vote Leave campaign though just because it was less odious comparatively. It was a work of manipulation and deception based on the best available market research and a shrewd understanding of mass psychology and how it can be used. Cummings appears to rather enjoy playing the pantomime villain, but this should not detract from the complicity of his more publicity-shy colleagues. Cummings spoke not merely for himself but for his cause, in all its scrupulous charm, when he allegedly told a parliamentary committee: 'Accuracy is for snake-oil pussies.'

It is too easy to blame a Rottweiler like Cummings for biting. When a fierce dog misbehaves, it is much the fault of its master or, in this case, masters: Boris Johnson, Michael Gove and all the Vote Leave high command are responsible for their campaign's distortions. They must live for ever with the consequences of their actions. Gove and Johnson commanded a wide degree of public trust, which exceeded the trust given to Cameron and Osborne, and abused it shamelessly and repeatedly.

There was scant fact-based defence for Leave claims like the cost of EU membership being £350 million a week, or 60 per cent of laws being made in Brussels. But this did not matter – it was win at all costs, and getting these myths across was a win–win for them. Cummings admitted the £350 million was a 'controversial claim', but continued to use it, after noticing how successfully it was picked up by the media. Martin Moore found that the *Express* repeated the £350 million claim no fewer than twenty-four times during the campaign, even though it had been conclusively proved false before it even appeared on the bus. Even if the numbers were easily debunked, it got the discussion onto the territory Leave wanted of alleged 'costs' and sovereignty. The bogey story about Turkey joining the EU – and the bogey story on stilts that the UK could not do anything about it – was another booby trap which, when touched by people who were attempting to debunk it, only spread the lies further.

No political campaign is completely honest, of course, but the Leave side put distortion at the centre of its entire strategy. Remain had some very bad moments, mostly connected with Osborne's threat of a 'punishment budget'. But in general its wrong calls were speculative predictions of instant economic meltdown rather than verifiably fact-free claims such as those peddled by Vote Leave.

The Vote Leave campaign organisers cannot escape the responsibility of picking the fruit of the poisoned tree that Farage planted and which the media and the Conservative right watered over the years. It should not have been the slightest bit surprising that things turned ugly after the referendum and we were pitched into a political climate of 'crush the saboteurs', 'silence EU whingers' and 'boycott the Remoaners'. Calling oneself a 'liberal Leaver' does not absolve a person of responsibility. One would almost rather have the brazen gloating of Arron Banks, self-proclaimed 'Bad Boy of Brexit', than the handwringing of some of his (de facto) fellow travellers on the journey to 'very well, alone and free' land.

The Leave campaign was at times overtly anti-rationalist, a disturbing development in any democratic society. Michael Gove's comment that 'people in this country have had enough of experts' may have been directed at poor reports from bodies like the IMF, but became deservedly notorious. But the shock is partly because Gove himself is a highly educated person of whom one can expect better. He and Boris Johnson cut and pasted into their new role their style as 'research-lite' newspaper columnists who exaggerate, understanding that they were living in a post-factual world, and if you said things in a persuasive enough way, enough people would believe you. Perhaps more revealing of the Leave movement's attitude towards facts is Nigel Farage's offhand observation that 'I think the doctors have got it wrong on smoking.' Never mind sixty years of scientific research: prejudice and self-indulgence are a better guide – belief is more important than evidence. Surely climate change is just another hoax dreamt up by scientists and university experts? A society that dismisses expertise is a society courting the prospect of book burning.

'The thing that you've got to remember with Michael is that he is basically a bit of a Maoist – he believes that the world makes progress through a process of creative destruction!', remarked Cameron once. Gove and his economic arguments for Brexit were condemned by Osborne as 'economically illiterate'. Gove has – like many of the Brexit leadership – lived in a self-reinforcing right-wing bubble of journalists, politicians and think-tank intellectuals. At least Gove's reservations about the EU were sincere, hence he escapes being a full 'guilty man'. But his abandonment of his two closest friends, Cameron and Osborne, is still troubling. When Gove abandoned Remain, Johnson followed. Bang went Britain in the EU.

Boris Johnson, in contrast, has always struggled with seriousness. Back in the old days when being casual about facts was considered an impediment in politics and even in journalism, Johnson was under a cloud, and tolerated as a buffoonish entertainer suited for the gaudier political offices like Mayor of London or as a periodic guest on *Have I Got News for You*. His long equivocations before joining the Leave campaign, to the point of drafting two contradictory articles about his position, should not be mistaken for soul-searching. One cannot but think, as did Cameron, that the highest ideal in his head was whichever action would best serve his personal career. Even after the vote Johnson appeared unsure of the consequences of what he had done, writing on 26 June in a piece of extraordinary wishful thinking or dishonesty:

> I cannot stress too much that Britain is part of Europe, and always will be ... EU citizens living in this country will have their rights fully protected, and the same goes for British citizens living in the EU.
>
> British people will still be able to go and work in the EU;

to live; to travel; to study; to buy homes and to settle down. As the German equivalent of the CBI – the BDI – has very sensibly reminded us, there will continue to be free trade, and access to the single market.

It took the expert stiletto (or perhaps, as cartoonist Peter Brookes suggested, sword) of Gove to kill off the danger of Johnson reaching No. 10. But then his career was miraculously revived. There are some places in government where glibness and charm can work quite well, but the office of Her Britannic Majesty's Secretary of State for Foreign and Commonwealth Affairs, as our burgundy passports declaim so grandly, is not one of them. In the original *Guilty Men*, Cato had a lot of fun with the 1936 appointment of Sir Thomas Inskip as Minister for Coordination of Defence; a man whose career had otherwise been mostly concerned with the legal profession and the 1928 prayer book controversy, was not a natural fit for the huge tasks at hand and a job that seemed a perfect fit for Winston Churchill. An eminent Churchillian – maybe the man himself – referred to it as 'the most cynical appointment since Caligula made his horse a consul'.

If nothing else, Cato the Younger can do something for Inskip's reputation. His appointment may have been incongruous and deeply cynical, but it is nothing on this metric compared to the pivotal job of Foreign Secretary being given to Boris Johnson.

But Johnson tells us he is a serious man. An honest man, and Britain will do much better in every way outside the EU. On this we hope the jester is right.

CHAPTER XIX

CRAPULENT CORBYN AND THE IMPLOSION OF LABOUR, 2015–2016

THE CAST:

Mr Jeremy Corbyn

SUPPORTING CAST:

Mr Seumas Milne, Mr John McDonnell

ALL WAS STILL NOT yet lost for Remain. Even if Tony Blair and Peter Mandelson were not the men to get Labour and traditional working class non-voters out, Gordon Brown, Alan Johnson, Sadiq Khan, Harriet Harman, David Miliband, Alistair Darling and a host of other respected Labour figures were on call. So whatever happened to them?

After the 2015 election, the upcoming EU referendum

gave Labour an opportunity, or responsibility, to help determine the course of the country for decades ahead. With the Tories wracked by internal divisions over Europe, the stage was set for Labour to walk on and play a leading role presenting a united front, a chance to restore its reputation as a credible and responsible national party; yet can in history a major party ever have produced a performance that bombed as abjectly?

In its 2015 manifesto, presided over by Ed Miliband, Labour's stance on Europe had been measured and committed. A clear economic case was made for membership, and the strength and influence that it offered Britain, even if it disappointed those who looked for a more positive tone about the EU. Labour promised to support reforms of EU governance to increase the role of national parliaments, to reform EU budgeting, and to have more restrictive immigration, social security and transitional controls. The referendum lock on further transfers of powers to Brussels was to be retained, but Miliband resisted the temptation to match Cameron's 'in–out' referendum call. The polls suggested it would have been to his electoral advantage, but Miliband was wary: it was 'an unnecessary gamble for our country,' he warned.

The dramatic defeat of Labour in May 2015 plunged the

party into a state of self-reflection and self-doubt. If it could not beat a Conservative Party after five years of unpopular, austerity-driven policies, when could it? Cameron's 'soft' conservatism had stolen the centre ground from them. It appeared a total nadir. Few could have foreseen that it was about to get worse.

When Miliband stood down, Andy Burnham was the favourite to succeed him. Little thought was given to Jeremy Corbyn's candidacy, a long-standing MP from the far left of the party who MPs backed to broaden the debate, but never to genuinely lead the party. Veteran New Labour strategist John McTernan was almost alone in calling these MPs 'morons'; the majority of them, and the public at large, thought it a harmless gesture, aimed at acknowledging the more radical roots of the party and including them in the debate. But the world had moved on, or back, to the early days of the Labour movement. Miliband had left a troubling and, it would prove, disastrous legacy.

The looming EU referendum played very little part in the Labour leadership campaign in the summer of 2015. Had it been otherwise, it would have been hard to elect Corbyn. He was a rare member of the Eurosceptic Labour tribe that was now a tiny minority in the modern party. It reflected neither

the views of other MPs nor of Labour members or supporters. As it was, however, spurred by a sudden mass movement
that defied all predictions, Corbyn was elected leader of the
Labour Party on Saturday 12 September, defeating Burnham,
Yvette Cooper and Liz Kendall.

At this pivotal moment in the nation's history, a decisive
Labour leader was urgently needed. As the referendum campaign gathered momentum, Corbyn's ambivalence to the EU
was to prove a huge handicap for Remain. He finessed as best
he could his long-established anti-EU position, giving the impression that he was reconciled to Europe, though it was to
come over as only damp praise. The seminal moment came
when he was asked on BBC One's *The Andrew Marr Show*
how he felt about the EU on a scale of one to ten, one weak
and ten very strong. Corbyn thought for a second. 'Seven, or
seven and a half,' he replied, shrugging his shoulders. It cap-
tured Corbyn perfectly: a ten for guileless honesty; a one for
statesmanlike leadership.

As interim leader in summer 2015, Harriet Harman had
recognised the need for Labour to get in gear with the campaign, and established the Labour In for Britain campaign
with former Cabinet minister Alan Johnson at its head. Its
separate identity from the all-party Remain effort reflected

the bruising experience of Better Together in Scotland before the Scottish referendum, which rendered Labour wary to the point of paranoia about cross-party organisations. Johnson was a popular and principled choice to lead it, and would later condemn Corbyn's inaction, claiming the Labour leadership 'undermined [Labour In's] efforts'. If the quirk of history had been different, and Cooper, Kendall, or Burnham had won the leadership election, the Labour In for Britain campaign would have received priority treatment. Some serious drive, money and sharpness would have been there to spur on the efforts of Johnson and his team.

Indeed, it is quite easy to imagine what an effective Labour In campaign might have looked like. The argument was clear, and one that the Conservatives could not make: there could have been a complementary relationship with No. 10 and the Conservative side of the campaign. While Cameron and Osborne concentrated on the economy, business and the world, Labour could have focused on European values and projects that soften the effects of globalisation, such as workers' rights, regional funding, fair trade and environmental protection. The trade unions had already managed to deter Cameron from negotiating away social protections in his February deal, and this could have paved the way for a committed endorsement of membership. The Tories' reputation for Euroscepticism, not least David Cameron's, severely limited their capacity to advocate for remaining; Labour's role was absolutely clear and crucial.

Labour's incapacity to mobilise the vote would prove fatal. Some of the strongest Leave votes came from former Labour heartlands. The formula for the campaign was that No. 10 would handle the polling, messaging and most of the air war, while Labour would fight the activist battles on the ground. But Corbyn and his supporters shunned the battle dress of the British army for that of the guerrilla. They were off fighting an entirely different war, for control over the Labour Party rather than for the future of the country; for winning the Labour argument rather than winning the European argument. Corbyn put his personal struggle ahead of the general good. Cato castigated Baldwin and Chamberlain for neglecting the national interest. Corbyn was their successor, a brother in arms.

Indeed, Corbyn's office was actively opposed to making a convincing case for Europe. They redrafted press statements to weaken their impact, fought battles to avoid giving even remote acknowledgement to Blair and Brown, failed to participate in conference calls and meetings and delayed crucial decisions. They complained about having to get up early to fight the most important campaign in recent history. Senior staff from the Remain campaign 'begged' Corbyn to take part in a rally with the Prime Minister. Even Gordon Brown was sent in to try to persuade him. But Corbyn utterly refused to be associated with Cameron, no matter how high the stakes. 'We can't stand there every week and wail away at you at PMQs and then get on stage with you,' said a senior Corbyn aide during a fraught meeting shortly before the vote. Lacking any clear direction from the top, many constituency Labour parties failed to deliver on the ground campaign. Just three weeks before the referendum vote nearly half of Labour voters were not aware of Labour's position. Many remained unsure, even at the end of the campaign. As a casebook study in political communication, this can have few equals for failure.

On 23 June 2016, two thirds of Labour voters (admittedly, a smaller Labour vote thanks to its hard-left turn) supported Remain. So far as the Labour leadership was concerned, this absolved them of responsibility. They could claim that more Labour voters supported Remain than the national average. Job done. But in truth it was a damning indictment. The fact that two thirds of Labour supporters could vote Remain

despite – not because of – Labour's restrained campaign
makes it easy to imagine a much larger chunk of voters being
persuaded by a more engaged, committed and enthusiastic
campaign from the top.

It would not have taken much. A better Labour campaign
simply required, at the very least, a figure who led convincingly with strong convictions. Corbyn believed his strategy was
mortally damaging the Conservatives, but a narrow Remain
vote delivered by Labour would have offered a greater political opportunity. It would have divided Cameron from many
of his own party. As it is, the Conservative Party became much
stronger. And those who Corbyn says he cares most about, the
least advantaged citizens in the UK, may well be those who
lose most from Brexit. Corbyn's children.

While Corbyn's director of communications, Seumas
Milne, and his shadow Chancellor, John McDonnell, emerge
as the main lieutenants, the leader who appointed them must
be ultimately responsible. Being leader of the Labour Party
in 2016 should have meant stepping up and fighting for the
settled policy of the Labour Party and most of the labour
movement which was to maintain Britain's membership of the
EU. Instead, Corbyn and his team have left those things they
care most about – the fate of workers' rights, the environment

and living standards – in the hands of the Tory Party. The shocking thing is that his people are not even sorry. Maybe they think that the 'harsh neo-Victorian climate of Brexit Britain,' as they see it, will create revolutionary consciousness among the proletariat. But the real victory for them is what they have always cared about most. The country? Forget it. Working people? Not so much. What they want is to retain control of the levers of power within the Labour Party.

They made a desert, and they call it momentum.

CHAPTER XX

BERLIN, BRUSSELS AND PARIS: FAILURE OF IMAGINATION (2015–2016)

THE CAST:

Frau Angela Merkel, M. Jean Claude-Juncker

SUPPORTING CAST:

M. François Hollande

THIRTY YEARS OF RELENTLESS artillery barrages fired across the English Channel from Fleet Street and Westminster at Berlin, Brussels and Paris have been excessive and poorly targeted. The EU and the most prominent national leaders within it have been easy targets, often diverting attention from where the real problems lay, on the home front. But that does not mean that they should escape responsibility altogether. Had Merkel, Juncker and Hollande acted differently in the year leading up to the referendum, Britain would not now be waiting impatiently in the departure lounge. All three bear deep culpability for any harm Britain's departure might yet do to prosperity and peace across Europe.

What is upsetting is that Merkel genuinely tried to understand Cameron and Britain's position. On 7 November 2012, she told Cameron at a private dinner at No. 10 she wanted to help him. But 'if Germany is seen to be too closely identified with Britain, then everything will be lost. I'm worried that Britain is the EU's "problem child", so work with me to mitigate this perception.' They were unusually close in 2012 and 2013, after their rocky start over his withdrawal from the EPP. It encouraged Cameron to think that she would do more to help the British position than she would. It was to prove a fatal miscalculation.

From 2014, Merkel began to run out of room for manoeuvre to help. The Eurozone crisis had damaged her. She was under pressure for insisting on tight fiscal austerity which prolonged the period of stagnation in the Eurozone to the detriment of Greece in particular, while the German economy itself was protected. While unemployment rose across the Eurozone, in Germany it fell, aided by its policy of undercutting its neighbours.

The Eurozone crisis was the inevitable result of the flawed

way the single currency was established in the 1990s. The prolonged and profound crisis from 2010 damaged faith in the competence of leaders of the EU as an institution. It resulted in an increase of migration into relatively prosperous Britain from depressed areas of the Continent. This put an intolerable strain upon the principle of free movement. Yet Merkel refused to acknowledge that the system was at fault: 'If the Euro fails, Europe fails.'

Merkel compounded her errors by her inflexibility on freedom of movement. Cameron was fully awake to the damage that migration into Britain was causing, and was panicked by the influx of refugees from Turkey, Syria and beyond into Greece and Italy from the summer of 2015 onwards. The EU failed to present a united response, or any sense of resolute leadership. The timing could not have been worse for No. 10, especially when terrorist attacks in Paris and Brussels were portrayed in the media as the result of EU migrants, and EU leaders seemed unable to staunch the attacks.

The architects of Schengen, like those of the euro, had failed to think about the long-term viability of their project, an error exposed mercilessly by the short-sightedness of EU leaders in the critical year from mid-2015. Merkel and Hollande refused to listen to Cameron's pleas for an emergency brake on migration into Britain from the EU, given the unusually high number the country was having to absorb. 'Germany will not tamper with the fundamental principles of free movement in the EU' Merkel declaimed in October 2014. Her Christian faith and first thirty-five years spent under communism in East Germany instilled in her an unshakeable sense of the right of freedom to cross borders. All she, Hollande, and Juncker were prepared to grant Cameron during the February 2016 renegotiation was an emergency brake on 'in-work' benefits for EU migrants, on top of the opt out from 'ever-closer union' and an exclusion from Euro-bailouts. This was a pittance when no less than a pound was required. The sadness is Merkel has been one of Germany's great Chancellors.

Hollande, in contrast, was a pale image of great French Presidents of the past. Considering his vain sexual dalliances, his lack of clarity and his inability to provide decisive leadership in France, it is hardly surprising that he lacked the imagination to support the British government's Remain quest. De Gaulle, even though he never wanted Britain to join, would have wanted to help Britain once in and work to devise the outer ring status after enlargement for nations like Britain, which by dint of their history, culture and economies could never be at the heart of Europe.

Juncker, likewise, paled in comparison with some of the great former EU Presidents such as Jenkins and Delors. Cameron knew Juncker would be hostile to Britain in any renegotiation, but believed he had won over Merkel's support to block Juncker's selection: another miscalculation. Juncker was elected President of the Commission in July 2014. The response from the British media was scathing: at sixty, he was way past his best, and they delighted in claims that he was renowned for drinking too much ('Junck the Drunk', or 'Jean-Claude Drunker' as several newspapers dubbed him). A better man than Juncker would have had the nous to keep Britain in Europe. But *nous* was not a quality that the EU excelled in during the critical year of its history in 2015–16.

It is Merkel though, for all her very considerable strengths and achievements, who bears the prime responsibility among EU leaders at the denouement. She prolonged the Eurozone crisis, exacerbated the migrant crisis – at least from a political perspective rather than a human one – and failed to give Cameron the emergency brake that would have made all the difference. 'No one will ever be able to prove the extent of the role played by Merkel's open border policies on the referendum's outcome,' wrote Jan Fleischhauer in *Der Spiegel*. 'But it can be considered certain that the images of huge groups of refugees making their way into Bavaria frightened many Brits. If the disciplined Germans are no longer willing or capable of protecting their borders, then who else is going to manage it?' Alexander Lambsdorff, the liberal Vice-President of the

European Parliament, is clear about her culpability: 'Brexit is also her responsibility', he said in the *Financial Times*.

Britain is to leave the EU because the positive case for membership was never clearly enough made and because the downsides were too easily distorted and presented endlessly to the British public. Perhaps the EU will be better off without awkward Britain. If so, Merkel, Hollande and Juncker will be seen as EU heroes for their work in engineering it.

Cameron will be blamed by many as the principal figure responsible for Brexit. The truth is not so simple, as this text makes clear. Britain leaving was the responsibility of many people over many years.

On 23 June, polling day, an internal poll seen in No. 10 gave the result as 55 to 45 in favour of Remain. The early results that night looked promising as Cameron and colleagues gathered around the television in No. 10. But as the night dragged on, the tables turned. The final result was 52 to 48 in favour of Leave. Just after 8 a.m., David Cameron came out to address the media in Downing Street.

The country has just taken part in a democratic exercise, perhaps the biggest in our history ... we should be proud of the fact that in these islands we trust the people for these big decisions ... The British people have voted to leave

the European Union and their will must be respected ...
There can be no doubt about the result ... I do not think it
would be right for me to try to be the captain that steers our
country to our next destination ... I love this country – and
I feel honoured to have served it.

Meanwhile, Donald Trump visiting his Trump International
Golf Course in Aberdeen, Scotland said he thought it was
a 'great thing' that the UK have 'taken back their country'.
Marine Le Pen, current leader of the far-right National Front
in France, described it as a 'victory for freedom! The British
people have given to Europeans and all the people of the
world a shining lesson in democracy.' Geert Wilders, leader of
the far-right Party for Freedom in the Netherlands, said he believed the end of the EU was now just a matter of time. Arron
Banks thought the referendum had been a good, fair contest:
'I don't give a monkey's ... we pushed the boundaries right to
the edge ... no one cares!' Hearing the result, Putin purred.
Nigel Farage declared that triumph had been achieved 'without a single bullet being fired'. He nevertheless told jubilant
supporters: 'I hope this victory brings down the failed project
... let June 23 go down in history as our Independence Day.'

Our Independence Day.

ENVOI

THE YOUNG SET OUT in their thousands from Cardiff, Coventy, Crieff, Coleraine and elsewhere across the UK, heading for the beaches and camps of southern Europe, not to sunbathe, but to assist the struggling masses fleeing Syria and beyond. Their grandfathers had fought in the Second World War, and their great-grandfathers in the First. They had fought for peace and freedom in Europe, of which Britain was an inseparable part.

Their young descendants came on the seventy-fifth anniversary of Dunkirk and they kept coming. They came because they wanted to help; because they saw in the weary children and broken adults – not aliens, foreigners nor cockroaches – but fellow and equal members of humanity.

The Britain of 2016 was very different to the Britain of 1940. Back then it did not stand alone, even before it was rescued by the US after 1941. It has become far more cosmopolitan, more connected, more liberal. The young are not alone in not wanting to swallow old men's archaic vision of British exceptionalism spiced with romantic, not to say strident, nationalism.

The idealism and optimism of the young has been sold short by the follies of some good men and women, and by the selfishness of some angry men who, for their own personal, financial or political gain, or for misplaced ideology, distorted the truth and paved the way for Britain to leave the EU. We will come through and we will thrive. There will be gains no doubt, and losses, from Britain leaving. But the hopes of so many young and not so young who overwhelmingly voted to remain in the EU, who are deeply proud of their country but also want to be part of a wider, peaceful fellowship of Europe in whose history Britain has always been entwined, has been diminished, perhaps for ever.

CHRONOLOGY

8 MAY 1945

Victory in Europe Day, celebrates the end of the Second World War following the surrender of Germany.

....

17 MARCH 1948

Treaty on Western Union (Brussels Pact) signed. Belgium, Britain, France, Luxembourg and the Netherlands form an alliance for mutual defence and economic cooperation.

....

9 MAY 1950

Schuman Plan announced.

....

19 APRIL 1951

European Coal and Steel Community (ECSC) treaty signed

in Paris by Belgium, France, Italy, Luxembourg, the Netherlands and West Germany.

....

25 MARCH 1957

Treaties of Rome instituting Euratom and the European Economic Community (EEC) signed by The Six.

....

7 JANUARY 1958

Walter Hallstein (Germany) becomes the first President of the
EEC Commission, which begins operations.

....

3 MAY 1960

European Free Trade Agreement (EFTA) formed by Austria, Denmark, Great Britain, Norway, Portugal, Sweden and Switzerland.

....

JULY-AUGUST 1961

Britain, Denmark and Ireland apply for EEC membership.

....

28 JANUARY 1963

France vetoes British membership.

....

8 APRIL 1965

Merger treaty signed. ECSC, EEC and Euratom are united in
the European Community (EEC).

....

NOVEMBER 27, 1967

De Gaulle blocks British membership again.

....

1 JULY 1968

Customs union begins.

....

1 JANUARY 1973

Britain, Denmark and Ireland join the EEC.

....

9-10 DECEMBER, 1974

European Council created by EEC leaders at Paris summit.

....

JANUARY 1977

Roy Jenkins (United Kingdom) becomes sixth President of the EEC Commission.

....

4-5 DECEMBER, 1978

European Council decides to introduce the EMS.

....

7-10 JUNE, 1979

First direct elections to the European Parliament.

....

1 JANUARY 1981

Greece becomes tenth member state of the EEC.

....

7 JANUARY 1985

Jacques Delors of France becomes eighth President of the EEC Commission.

....

1 JANUARY 1986

Portugal and Spain officially enter the Community.

....

18 AND 28 FEBRUARY 1986

Single European Act signed in Brussels.

....

20 SEPTEMBER 1988

In her Bruges speech, Margaret Thatcher warns of a European 'superstate'.

....

19 NOVEMBER 1989

Fall of the Berlin Wall.

....

19 JUNE 1990

Schengen Agreement signed.

....

7 FEBRUARY 1992

Maastricht Treaty on European Union signed.

....

20 SEPTEMBER 1992

French narrowly approve Maastricht Treaty; vote is preceded by chaos on the financial markets leading to elimination of the pound sterling from the EMS.

....

18 MAY 1993

Danes vote 'yes' to Maastricht after initial rejection.

....

28-29 JULY 1993

Near collapse of EMS.

....

26 MARCH 1995

Schengen free movement begins.

....

26 JULY 1995

Europol Convention signed. Begins work in October 1998.

....

1 JANUARY 1999

The single currency, the euro, enters operation and will be available in note form from 1 January 2002.

....

15 MARCH 1999

European Commission resignations following the publication
of a report on fraud, wasteful management, and cronyism. Several commissioners, including Edith Cresson, a former Prime
Minister of France, are criticised by name.

....

MAY 2003

Eastern European accession occurs, making twenty-five members.

....

JUNE 2004

Constitutional treaty is agreed but rejected by France and
Holland in 2005 via referendum.

....

12 SEPTEMBER 2006

Nigel Farage wins UKIP leadership contest.

....

JANUARY 2007

Accession of Bulgaria and Romania. Now twenty-seven
members.

....

DECEMBER 2007

Treaty of Lisbon is signed.

....

21 DECEMBER 2007

Schengen area is enlarged to include Estonia, the Czech Republic, Lithuania, Hungary, Latvia, Malta, Poland, Slovakia and Slovenia.

....

12 JUNE 2008

Ireland rejects the Treaty of Lisbon in a referendum, approves it 3 October with second referendum.

....

1 DECEMBER 2009

The Lisbon Treaty comes into effect.

....

7 MAY 2010

Together with the IMF, EU leaders approve emergency funding worth up to €750 billion to bail out members of the Eurozone unable to finance their national debt.

....

23 JANUARY 2013

David Cameron promises a referendum on EU membership.

....

APRIL 2015

The start of the European migrant crisis.

....

5 SEPTEMBER 2015

Merkel announces there will be 'no limits on the number of asylum seekers' Germany will take in. Over 476,000 asylum applications were registered in Germany in 2015, with officials putting the total number of arrivals at over a million.

....

16 JUNE 2016

Jo Cox, Labour MP and Remain campaigner, is tragically killed.

....

23 JUNE 2016

Britain votes 52 per cent to 48 per cent to leave the EU.

....

APPENDIX

THE WARNING FROM
CATO THE YOUNGER

CATO PROAVUS ABHINC ANNOS LXX, cum
Germani isto scelesto duce armis antecedere vellent, libro suo
viros quindecim culpavit qui Britannos haud satis de periculo
monuissent.

duo consulares illo libro obruti sunt; in quo tamen nihil de
imbellium fautore quodam dictum est. eo tempore sim-
plicius vivebatur. Cato enim cum hostium facinora facile
oppugnabat tum viros castigabat qui consilium difficile
ceperunt; quod quidem minus inepte factum postea visum
est. dum autem in dubio manebat eventus, salutare erat
aliquos culpare.

nec hodie, quamvis latentior sit culpa, dubitari potest quin
duces nostri in re Concilii Europaei inepte, corrupte, debiliter

egerint. pietate igitur moveor ad scribendum, ut errore deposito meliora persequamur.

nos Britanni nunc multis post annis e Concilio sumus discessuri. nolo omnes castigare qui talia commendaverunt: erant in utraque parte boni viri, consilia bona. quindecim tamen noxios habeo, quorum crimina vel graviora vel leviora haec sunt:

(i)   fallacia

(ii)   simulatio

(iii)   captura

(iv)   malo ductu

(v)   arrogantia

de officio quo ibi fungimur diu disputatur, sed pessime; Concilium in actis diurnis detrectari solet, scilicet ut delectentur lectores; neque inter duces nostros exstiterunt defensores.

Europaei interea duces se praebuere deteriores, nescientes quomodo eos sodales tractent qui adesse quam praeesse malint. Ubi nunc illi auctores studiosi? Dum consilio ingenio opus erat, omnia minutiis impediebantur.

defensores ducesque deerant. Victu breviter periclitante aderat plebicola. Suffragium poscebatur. De discessu facile constitutum est; quod tamen nullo modo necessarium erat. Cato proavus noxios facilius culpavit quod, ubi spes pacis irrita fuit, haud bene parati bellum gerere coacti sumus. Hoc tamen anno, postquam e Concilio discedere constituimus, cladem de qua monebamur nondum accepimus. Nec non et si peiora sequentur, ei qui discessum urgebant adversarios suos, non se ipsos, castigabunt: sic maxime erunt noxii.

consilium sapientius adhuc inveniri potest. Concilium enim ipsum serius ocius corrigendum erit; quod, si manere constituissemus, nos incitare potueramus. Nunc tamen spectare debebimus; aliorum erit varietatem cum concordia restituere.

libellum lamentationum non habes, lector: nam speramus Britannos post discessum valituros, omnes Europaeos in hoc saeculo pacem abundantiamque habituros esse.

ubicumque bonum sine periculo capi potest, nobis iuxta Concilium Europaeum aliqua manendum est. culpam eorum quos proavus castigavit duces fortes postea redemerunt; quod iterum et semper accidere potest.